GARDENING IN MINIATURE

ALSO BY ROY GENDERS

BULBS: A COMPLETE HANDBOOK
THE ROSE
COLOUR ALL THE YEAR ROUND
COVERING A WALL
PLANTING FRUIT TREES

ROY GENDERS

GARDENING IN MINIATURE

LONDON
ROBERT HALE & COMPANY
63 Old Brompton Road, S.W.7

First published in Great Britain 1958
Second edition 1975

ISBN 0 7091 4583 7

Printed and bound in Great Britain by
REDWOOD BURN LIMITED
Trowbridge & Esher

CONTENTS

LIST OF ILLUSTRATIONS

GARDENING IN MINIATURE

Chapter 1

GARDENING IN MINIATURE

The new trend in gardening – The intimacy of a small garden – The town garden – The roof garden – Maintenance of the small garden – A water garden.

THE post-war migration of the countryman to the town and the high cost of labour making it impossible for all but the wealthiest to maintain a large garden, has brought about an entirely new conception of gardening. With the Englishman's love of a garden being just as strong today as ever it was, the large garden of the country house has become the miniature garden of the town house and the plant raiser has been quick to recognize this change. A new series of plants of both annual and perennial form has been developed to replace those once used for large beds and borders and which required considerable labour with their upkeep and a large outlay for their planting. The new annuals grow to a height of between 4–9 in., are of most compact habit and remain long in bloom with little or no attention. Many annuals may be raised without heat which has now become uneconomic for the amateur to use and so the trend is to grow the more hardy plants. The need for the miniature garden to be as colourful as possible has also brought about a demand for a plant to bear a large amount of bloom however dwarf it might be and one which will remain in bloom over a long period. The high wages of labour and the fact that the continued rising cost of living makes ever-increasing demands upon the time of most people, means that the garden lover must tend his (or her) own garden, though time for recreation is limited. It is therefore necessary for the garden to be as labour saving as possible, staking and tying being reduced to a minimum as well as the planting and cleaning of beds. Only those plants having a compact, sturdy habit should be grown, not only to make staking unnecessary but so that as many plants as possible may be planted into a very small area to give the maximum amount of colour. Inter-planting, using winter and spring flowering plants followed by those which bloom through summer and autumn in the same bed, will do much to reduce lifting and cleaning of the ground. The concentration of plants of dwarf habit into small beds has seen the modern garden become more colourful than could have been contemplated a decade ago, whilst our gardening has become more intimate. We now tend the plants ourselves and can better appreciate a display of great beauty in return for our labours. There are plants to suit every pocket and every garden, however small. Even where there is no garden, much enjoyment may be obtained from a window box, a tub or trough, there now being many varieties of plants suitable for this style of gardening. To obtain the best results, however, calls for careful preparation of the soil and selection of plant to suit both climate and situation. Even the back yard may be converted into a most colourful courtyard where may be planted a shrubbery, a rose border or where a small rockery may be made. Or more simply, hanging baskets fixed to the walls, or of troughs or tubs arranged along several sides of a yard, will provide

colour almost the whole year round. Because there may be no garden to the property does not mean that one cannot be made quite simply and inexpensively, depending upon the size of the yard and upon the time at one's disposal for its eventual upkeep. Some of the most charming and colourful little gardens, which may well be called miniature gardens and which were once ugly back yards or flat roofs, are now to be found in the centre of most of our industrial cities. They are entirely labour saving and most inexpensive to maintain. No mechanical tools are required, the only tools required being a stainless steel trowel, possibly a small border fork and perhaps a small pair of shears.

It is quite possible to bring glimpses of the country to a small town garden or courtyard and one of the most delightful the author has seen was situated to the rear of a London mews house, the area measuring only 20 ft. × 15 ft. To the centre, two or three silver birch trees were growing, having been planted 3 ft. apart, primroses and dwarf bulbs being planted around the base which was surrounded by crazy paving stone. Around this was made a small border filled with dwarf shrubs and herbaceous plants set in groups, to present a most natural appearance. Amongst the shrubs were planted miniature bulbs and winter flowering heathers, which added to the almost dell-like atmosphere of this once ugly town back yard and there was colour throughout the year.

The Intimacy of a Small Garden

It is surprising how colourful a tiny garden can be made, due to the concentration of colour in so small an area. In comparison, a large garden presents a picture of sparse beauty, rather than one of concentrated richness. A group of *Iris reticulata* for instance, and two or three plants of the winter flowering polyanthus, Barrowby Gem would hardly make their presence felt in a large garden, yet in one of tiny proportions, their fullness of beauty would be clearly revealed. In a miniature garden it is possible to focus attention on the smallest of plants and to appreciate all they have to offer, whereas in a large garden they would most likely go entirely unnoticed. A single plant of that brilliantly coloured primrose, Sunset Glow with its orange-red flowers or of viola, Bullion with its golden-yellow blooms, would bring to life the darkest corner of a miniature-sized garden whereas it would be quite lost in the large garden.

The smaller the garden, the more intimate one may become with the plants, with their form and character, each one revealing qualities so often overlooked where the garden is large and where the whole panorama may be appreciated rather than the individual characteristics of the plants. It is also possible in a limited area, to give the plants that additional care in their culture that would be quite impossible in a large garden and it is amazing how they will respond. Those who have been able to give additional care to the dainty violettas, removing dead blooms as they form, working peat around their "crowns" during summer and feeding with liquid manure to enhance the display, will be rewarded with a greatly extended display and a greater freedom of flowering than thought possible where the plants are allowed to look after themselves. A few minutes in the garden in the evening or before breakfast on all suitable occasions is all that is necessary to maintain the plants in health and vitality when they will repay one a thousandfold for any additional time spent on them.

The Town Garden

A small town garden will generally permit the growing of the less hardy plants, due to the provision of more shelter from cold winds and severe frost, the walls of a yard or house, though possibly reducing the amount of sunshine, acting as an efficient windbreak. It is cold winds which cause the most trouble to plants, especially those which bloom in winter and spring. Protection will also enable the more tender plants, e.g. the multiflora begonias, to be planted out a week or ten days earlier than permissible where planted in a more exposed bed, whilst generally for the same reason, the display will be extended for the same length of time. Against this advantage, however, is the need for the plants of a town garden to be able to withstand deposits of soot and sulphur and where particularly concentrated, it will be better to use only those plants which either die back in winter, which most of the hardy border plants do, or those which occupy the ground for only a short time, though this may not be practical where time for gardening is strictly limited. But not all small gardens are situated in the midst of industrial towns, for many country cottages and especially country houses built since the war, possess only a very small garden which may be augmented by the use of old stone troughs. Here may be grown those plants which do not take too kindly to town gardens, the violet and pink being at their best in a clean atmosphere and in a soil which is in no way acid. Plants for the seaside garden should also be able to withstand salt laden winds, which a number of plants and flowering shrubs, though of dwarf habit, are not able to do.

The Roof Garden

The exposed roof garden will provide quite different conditions than those provided by a walled garden. The plants will be required to withstand the full rays of the summer sun which may often be intense, whilst the plants will receive little or no protection from frost and cold winds. This will mean that only the very hardiest of the winter and spring flowering plants should be grown and for the summer those able to withstand dry conditions and in this respect members of the geranium family will prove most suitable.

A roof garden may be paved or it may originally have been made of concrete in which case tubs, ornamental vases and "window" boxes may be artistically used. Those containing conifers and the more tender trees and shrubs could be moved to a sheltered corner during winter, and it may be possible to erect a low wooden screen to protect them from cold winds. Where space permits, they may instead be taken indoors and taken out again early in spring. The use of one or more deciduous trees to provide some shade from the ummer sun will add to the value of the roof garden for those wishing to make use of it for relaxation, also to its appearance whilst at the same time providing flowering plants with some shade. A small water garden and fountain will give added charm to the garden.

Maintenance of the Small Garden

Manure now being a scarce commodity, it is convenient that the more dwarf plants are well able to bloom to perfection with the minimum amount. Hops, shoddy and peat, all clean to handle will prove just as efficient as farmyard manure and will be more readily obtained. Watering too, presents few difficulties with a small garden even during a period of drought. For one thing, being protected from the sun's rays by a high wall or the walls of a house or outbuilding, the soil does not dry out so quickly and where carefully prepared before planting, only during a prolonged drought will the plants require artificial moisture. Also, where the garden is of very small proportions, pest and disease may be kept under more complete control. The usual pests of the large country garden, rabbits and wood pigeons will be absent, but slugs and house sparrows will be encountered instead. It is, however, much easier to protect groups of plants set out closely together in small beds rather than where scattered over a large area.

In the small garden, the use of stone may be considerably more effective, adding not only to the appearance of the garden but being an aid to one's gardening, making it possible to pursue one's hobby when the weather is anything but kind. The economical use of stone in the form of crazy paving or cement paving stones as an alternative to grass will, in the small town garden be a great asset. Once laid, and this should be done correctly over a concrete base as fully described in a later chapter of this book, the stones will prove permanent and will require no attention apart from an occasional sweeping with a hard brush to remove soil and to prevent the formation of moss. There will be no cutting as so necessary with grass, whilst the stone will in no way be troubled by the acid forming desposits of the atmosphere, as grass so often is in a town. The original outlay is, however, greater where stone is used though against this and apart from its efficiency, a small area may be made to look more attractive in a much quicker time.

A small area may, however, be made to become most pleasing by using the more simple designs. The transforming of one ugly town yard into a miniature dell garden has already been described, but for those who prefer symmetry and have the very minimum of time to attend their garden, more simple suggestions can be made. A centre piece of paving surrounded by slightly raised beds to be filled with spring and later with summer bedding plants may be inexpensively maintained. Perhaps around the garden could be planted those conifers of most compact, upright habit to give winter colour and to help hide an unsightly wall. The green of the conifers will be accentuated if the walls are treated with Snowcem. This is a cement preparation and does not flake off as does ordinary whitewash. It is advisable to treat all inside walls so that the white finish will enable the maximum amount of sunlight to be reflected to the beds for the one great difficulty with a town yard to be converted to a garden is that, especially where facing north or east, sunlight is excluded by high walls and buildings.

Where the plants are likely to be deprived of sunlight, then only those which are known to flourish in shade or in partial shade should be planted, the sun lovers such as the pink and begonia being excluded. Most of the bulbs and spring flowering plants will tolerate almost full shade, whilst there are a number of trees and shrubs of dwarf habit which will flourish under such conditions. A garden facing full sun would, however small, be made more pleasing and would be more easily managed if one or two neatly growing trees were to be planted. These could be made the focal point around which the garden was to be planned. A flowering cherry, weeping willow, maple or silver birch would prove suitable and with their colourful bark and twigs, would remain attractive during winter.

As an alternative, a garden ornament could be used, not one of those brilliantly coloured gnomes or mushrooms, but an ornamental vase which could be filled with flowering plants of neat trailing habit, or a sundial, made with imitation "stone" bricks. With the Dry Pack Concrete stone maker, priced only 19s. 6d., as many as three dozen imitation "stone" bricks can be made in an hour at a cost of less than a penny each. These bricks are useful for making all manner of attractive garden ornaments as well as low walls (described later) and steps, which will bring charm to the most uninteresting of small gardens. Or a small rustic bird table could be obtained or a cote for fan-tail pigeons.

Round wooden tubs or those made of concrete bricks and square in shape to accommodate miniature conifers or flowering shrubs are also attractive about a yard or roof garden and may be used where it is not desired to have any ground beds. Used with taste they will provide continuous beauty for the very minimum of attention. Tubs may also be used to make a most attractive miniature water garden and they have the advantage over a concrete pond in that a tub is not so permanent and where it may not come up to original expectations, it may easily be replaced.

A Water Garden

A more permanent water garden, stocked with water lilies and attractive marginal plants may be enhanced by a fountain. The Stokes fountain, which is able to utilize a 6in. depth of water over and over again and is extremely inexpensive to run, will transform the most ordinary small garden into one of continental beauty. It works by electricity, the cable being connected from a power point to the fountain. Where it is necessary to carry the cable across a lawn or border, it should be encased in metal tubing at a depth of 18 in. as a safeguard against cutting it whilst performing garden operations. The fountain will throw a jet up to 6 ft. in height and running water is not necessary.

A small pool may easily be constructed on a lawn or in a paved courtyard to a depth of 12 in., a greater depth being unnecessary both for the working of the fountain and the maintenance of plant life. A rectangular pool will be more easily made, first making the sides quite straight and perpendicular. A layer of concrete to a depth of 2 in. should first be placed over the floor and when set quite firm, a wooden frame should then be placed over. This should have been made to dimensions 1 in. less than that of the excavated opening and should be 10 in. in height to bring it to the level of the surrounding ground. Into the aperture between the frame and sides, the concrete is poured, the frame being removed when set hard. Be sure to allow a small opening near the top of the pool by which the cable may be connected to the fountain. This may be made before the concrete becomes fully set. Around the sides of the pool crazy paving stone set into concrete will give the pond a more attractive appearance, the top of the stone protruding slightly above the edge of the pond. This will be filled with plants as described in Chapter II, the fountain being placed on a stone so that the nozzle will be protruding just above the level of the water.

Where the garden is to be as labour saving as possible, it may be covered entirely with pre-cast concrete flagstones, cemented together and leaving only a few corners free of cement in which carpeting plants may be planted to give the area a less bleak appearance. Or crazy paving stones may be used, using as large sized stones as possible and laying them on a bed of cement to prevent perennial weeds and grass from appearing through where the stones are cemented together. About the paving may be placed troughs or tubs filled with miniature plants and trees and to give colour the whole year round. An ornamental tree of neat habit could be planted to provide shade and beneath which one may relax in comfort, whilst it would also take away much of the somewhat harsh appearance of the stone.

An unsightly corner may be transformed by placing several tubs containing conifers around the walls and to the front placing a wooden garden seat. Or as an alternative to the cupressus trees, a weeping willow may be planted in a tub and placed where two walls may meet. A few additional tubs for flowering plants arranged about the courtyard would create a most pleasing appearance from what was once an ugly back yard.

A most attractive small garden may be made by dividing into two an area of about 20 ft. × 15 ft. by means of a brick path 15–16 in. wide, the bricks, if possible of old appearance, being placed on their side in a bed of concrete, the uppermost side of the bricks being made level with each other and with the surrounding ground. Each half of the garden may be divided into a number of rectangular or

circular beds of similar size and shape and planted with miniature roses, pathways of white gravel which has been washed, or of turf dividing the beds. A miniature garden so constructed would be a lasting tribute to one's skill and would be permanent and labour saving. Where space permits, a miniature box "hedge" could be used to advantage to surround the beds or to plant alongside the path. It would give protection to the more tender plants where used, such as the multiflora begonias as well as being evergreen throughout the year.

Should there be no garden, only a small area which has been concreted or asphalted and which it is not desired to disturb in any way, troughs may be used to provide colour and interest, whilst hanging baskets may be suspended from the high walls, which generally surround a back yard. Made up during the first days of May, the baskets will prove colourful from mid-June until mid-November, provided they are never allowed to suffer from lack of moisture and dead blooms are occasionally removed. Or "window" boxes may be fixed to a wall and planted exactly as where used for window display.

An unsightly corner could be made most attractive by means of a small rockery, a mound of soil and stones so constructed as to hide a dust-bin or the lower part of the wall of an unsightly outhouse. The use of miniature bulbs and flowering plants would provide colour throughout the year. There is no reason at all why a small, ugly back yard of a town house should not be made most attractive for the minimum of outlay and attention. The larger garden too may be made more interesting by dividing it, by means of wattle hurdles or neat dwarf hedges, into a number of small gardens and making each entirely different in character.

Chapter 2

THE MINIATURE ROSE GARDEN

Making a miniature rose garden – Propagation – Varieties – Dwarf floribundas.

However small the garden, the Englishman's love of his national flower is such that a place must generally be found for a rose bed, however small. Those with a large garden will have room to grow the vigorous Peace and those wonderful varieties such as Tzigane, Tahiti and Grand Gala, all of similar habit and having Peace as a parent. More like shrubs than rose bushes, they require ample space in which to grow, likewise many of the more vigorous floribunda and polyantha roses which often attain a height of 4-5 ft. For the average sized garden, the more compact of the hybrid tea roses may be accommodated, varieties such as Ena Harkness, Charles Gregory and Eden Rose.

Making a Miniature Garden

Those having a very small garden, possibly only a small courtyard surrounded by a narrow raised border or even where there is no garden whatsoever, a trough or window box providing the only means of colour, may also enjoy their roses. Requiring little attention and remaining long in bloom, the quite inexpensive miniature roses are extremely hardy and long lasting and require nothing elaborate in their culture. The plants are of so neat a habit that they may be used to make the tiniest rose garden it is possible to imagine. Small pieces of crazy paving stone may be used to divide the ground into sections of the required design, the stone being used as a pathway, though it should not be more than 6–8 in. wide to keep it in correct scale with the miniature rose trees. Strips of grass, formed by laying turf or sowing seed, may be used as an alternative method of laying out the tiny garden and will be kept neat by clipping with shears.

The size of the rose garden will depend upon available space, but a sunny corner of a garden, however small will prove suitable, whilst the miniature roses are most attractive used to make a "rose garden" in a trough. There are now miniature standard roses which greatly adds to the charm of the garden and to obtain the best effect, tiny "hedges" of evergreen box and dwarf conifers may be used.

Most attractive is the dwarf juniper *Communis compressa* which forms a pencil-like tree only 6–9 in. high, its feathery glaucous green foliage making a pleasing foil for the roses.

Where a miniature rose garden is being made, it is important to keep everything to scale, using the most dwarf varieties for a trough or window box and where space in the garden is at a premium. These grow only 8–9 in. tall and separate varieties or colours may be planted to each bed; or they are most attractive planted in a small raised circular bed, surrounded by a path of crazy paving or by a tiny "hedge" of dwarf box. These delightful little roses may also be used to edge a bed of the more compact of the hybrid tea and polyantha roses where room permits the use of these more vigorous roses. They may also be planted about a rockery in groups of three or four together with the dwarf junipers. At all times they require a position of full sun but they do like a soil which does not allow their roots to dry out and so the plants almost always flourish when planted on a rockery, where pockets of soil between the stones may be prepared by the addition of humus-forming materials.

Plants used in a trough or window box or to make up a small bed or garden in the open will require the same attention as to soil conditions, the addition of leaf mould or peat augmented by some well-decayed manure, especially cow manure, being necessary to maintain summer moisture. Only dry conditions at their roots will harm the plants, neither frost nor cold winds causing them trouble. An excess of manure, however, should not be given or the plants will form too much foliage at the expense of bloom. If a little decayed manure cannot be obtained, incorporate 2 oz. of bone meal to each square yard of ground and a similar amount where a trough garden is being made. If a little Kettering loam, yellow and fibrous, can be obtained, so much the better, but apart from these simple requirements, the plants need nothing more. It is, however, important to see that they do not suffer from lack of moisture during summer, whilst an occasional application of weak manure water, obtainable in concentrated form in bottles from any sundriesman will do much to enhance the bloom and prolong the display.

The miniature roses seem to resent root disturbance more than other roses and so pot-grown plants should be used whenever possible. Plants from pots will become more quickly established and may be planted at any time except when the soil is frozen, though possibly October or March will be the most suitable months to make a miniature rose garden. The plants should of course be removed from their pots or they will suffer from lack of moisture.

When planting, place the ball of compost holding the roots just below soil level, for shoots which appear from below the ground will also bear bloom. These should be cut back halfway each autumn, likewise any unduly long or decayed shoots to maintain the shape and health of the tree. Also, to prolong the display, apart from occasional feeding, all dead bloom should be removed as it forms. This will also keep the plants compact and tidy. The plants should be allowed sufficient room to develop for though they will not grow tall, they will spread out in bush-like fashion and will grow as wide as they grow tall, which will be about 9 in.

Propagation

The plants may be readily increased by cuttings taken during early autumn and inserted in a sandy compost. The new season's shoots should be used, taking cuttings about 3 in. in length and trimming to a leaf bud. They will root more readily if the base of the shoots are treated with hormone powder before inserting round the sides of pots or pans. They may also be planted in frames or under cloches. Plant firmly and keep the compost comfortably moist, shading the shoots should strong sunshine be experienced before rooting has taken place. As soon as the cuttings have formed roots, they should be potted separately into 3-in. pots and grown on until ready to be planted out the following spring, pinching out the growing point to encourage bushy growth. Clean, fibrous loam containing a little sand for drainage is all that is required for growing on the plants in pots whilst the roots must never be allowed to lack moisture.

Miniature roses may also be quite easily raised from seed and though not coming true to name, some lovely varieties may be raised in this way. A good strain of *Rosa polyantha nana*, which is the name for the Fairy Rose, may be obtained for half a crown a packet which will give about a dozen plants. Seed should be sown in boxes or pans containing the John Innes Sowing Compost, the time to sow being from mid-April to mid-May. The compost should be kept moist and the seed shaded until germination takes place, which may be slow in comparison with most seeds. If growing outdoors, cover the box with a piece of glass until the seed has germinated.

The seedlings should be transplanted to small pots containing a good loamy soil to which a little leaf mould has been incorporated and they should be kept comfortably moist. They will have formed plants suitable for setting out by the following spring or early summer.

Varieties

There are now many charming variations of the miniature or fairy rose, embracing almost every known colour so that there is something to suit every taste. New and quite unusual is Baby Faurax, which grows only 10 in. tall and bears masses of tiny pale blue flowers of semi-double form. No other rose bears a bloom nearer to the true blue colouring.

One of the loveliest varieties is Josephine Wheatcroft which bears a tapering bloom of true hybrid tea form, the size of a shilling and of a lovely shade of rich buttercup yellow, ideal for table decoration or as a button hole. As it grows to a height of about 15–16 in. it should not be used for a trough or tiny garden, but is best planted in a small circular bed to itself.

The other fairy roses bear a bloom similar to those of the polyantha roses, button shaped. The habit of the plant too, is similar and they may more accurately be described as miniature polyantha roses. Outstanding is Baby Masquerade, the pale yellow blooms being splashed with red, whilst equally lovely are the large deep pink blooms of Tinker Bell. Most attractive when planted together are Maid Marion, with its double crimson button-like blooms; and the double white, edged pink Cinderella, which grows to a height of 9 in. Equally free flowering is Humpty Dumpty, glistening pink; and Sweet Fairy, the blooms being of a pleasing shade of mauve-pink and very full. Both varieties are very dwarf.

A lovely new introduction, making a plant about 9 in. tall is Presumida, bearing circular fully double blooms of rich apricot, edged with gold. Baby Gold Star, of similar height, and with its blooms of a deep buttercup yellow, is also lovely; also the true guinea gold, Rosina. Of those of taller habit, is Perle de Montserrat, its blooms being of a peach-pink colour. Of those of more dwarf habit and most suitable for a trough garden or the rockery, in addition to Sweet Fairy is Mon Petit, with its blooms of deep rose-pink; Pixie, pure white; and Twinkles, shell-pink. They are extremely dwarf and are most dainty.

Of similar habit to Josephine Wheatcroft is the striking Perle d'Alcanada with its tiny hybrid tea blooms of deep carmine-red, whilst the lovely creamy-white Pour Toi has similar glossy foliage and also grows to a height of 9 in. Two new varieties of polyantha form are Granada, blood red and Red Imp, crimson. They are extremely showy either as bushes or standards, in which form they reach a height of 16 ins. and are most attractive planted at the centre of a small bed or trough. The stems should be supported with a neat cane.

Dwarf Floribundas

A new series of miniature roses of slightly larger habit are the first true dwarf floribundas which grow to a height of from 14–16 in.

and form bushes almost as wide as they grow tall. These are the Walt Disney Compacta roses, the bloom being borne in trusses rather than singly. With their glossy green foliage they are well able to withstand the most adverse weather and are ideal plants for along the top of a terrace or wall, or for planting in raised beds where their rich colouring may be appreciated to the full. They are also most attractive when used to border a small path and for planting in almost any position about a very small garden.

Possibly the outstanding variety is Grumpy, which bears a large cup-shaped bloom of vivid scarlet, whilst of similar form is Sneezy, the bloom having a white centre. With its blooms of geranium-red, Bashful is most striking, whilst Doc and Sleepy bear semi-double blooms of deep rose-pink. As yet there is no yellow flowered variety, but a most compact floribunda bearing golden-yellow blooms is Goldilocks which grows to a height of only 18–20 in. and is excellent for bedding in the very small garden. Of similar habit, the double yellow blooms having an attractive apricot tint is Yellow Pinocchio. Both may be planted at the centre of a bed and surrounded with Bashful or Grumpy for a display of great brilliance.

There are a number of floribunda and polyantha roses of most compact habit which makes them ideal for a small garden for planting in beds or they may be used, like the Compacta roses along a terrace or wall. Of the floribundas, the new scarlet Concerto; the clear pink flowered Fairy Princess and Fashion, with its clusters of pure salmon coloured flowers are of compact habit and have attractive deep-glossy green foliage. Only slightly taller and of great brilliance of colour is De Ruiter's Herald, the flowers being pillar-box-red, whilst the plant is extremely disease resisting.

Of the polyantha roses whose habit it is not possible to determine when the bloom is displayed on the show bench, many are very tall growing and suitable only for the largest of gardens, some are of medium height, whilst a few grow to a height of no more than 18–20 in. and may be used with confidence in a very small garden. Outstanding is Wheatcroft's Golden Polyantha, the fully double blooms being of deepest yellow and is the best variety of its colour. Of those bearing a pink flower, Little Dorrit, which bears masses of pale-shell-pink button-like blooms; and Coral Cluster, of similar habit and bearing beautiful coral-pink blooms are most charming. A magnificent variety is Cameo. Of very dwarf habit, its coral-pink blooms are flushed with orange. Ideal bears a truss of deepest crimson, whilst the older Paul Crampel bears a bloom of geranium-red, hence its name. Of similar colouring is Pompone Beauty, whilst the dainty Posy which grows only 16 in. tall and bears clusters of rose-red flowers must not be forgotten.

Of the hybrid tea roses suitable for a very small garden, though they cannot truly be called miniatures by any means, Picture bears a bloom of a glorious shade of shell-pink delicately flushed with orange. Shot Silk, of similar but less delicate colouring; Lady Belper, buff-apricot; Golden Dawn, moonlight-yellow; and the crimson-red, Etoile de Hollande are all suitable for a small garden where the maximum colour is required from the smallest area.

It is rarely that a rose border is seen in the modern garden, but with the rose being so labour saving a plant, a miniature border of roses would be a welcome alternative to a herbaceous border or small shrubbery. One method of making a border of miniature roses and which brought great charm to the tiny, sunny courtyard of the author's garden, was to build on the sunny side a low stone wall 2 ft. above ground level and 3 ft. from the high walls surrounding the yard. This was filled with fibrous loam and planted with roses, the dwarf polyantha and floribunda roses at the back, with the Walt Disney Compacta roses to the front. The row immediately in front consisted of those fairy roses which grow to a height of about 12 in., with the most dwarf in front. The four rows ranging in height from 6 in. to almost 2 ft., provide a bank or border of brilliant colour from June until almost the year end, the plants being sheltered from adverse weather by the surrounding walls which should be whitewashed to reveal the full beauty of the bloom.

A rose border, using plants of similar height may be made in any small garden, planting along one side or around a small lawn or around a centre of crazy paving stones. The fairy roses are equally attractive planted in front of a terrace or low wall, the taller varieties to the back with the true miniature roses in front. The miniatures are amongst the easiest plants to manage and should be more widely used where conditions restrict the planting of the more vigorous types.

Chapter 3

ANNUALS FOR SMALL BEDS

The new dwarf annuals and their use – Raising the plants – Annuals for summer bedding.

UNTIL quite recently the range of summer flowering annual plants having a neat, compact habit was extremely small, for gardening had not become so intimate as it has today, the window box and miniature town garden having replaced the large garden and the professional gardener. At one time, plants were required to give as robust a display as possible, the need to spend considerable time on their staking and tying being given little or no consideration. Today, these conditions have changed entirely, most gardens being small, many extremely so, whilst window box and tub gardening have taken on a new interest. The plant raiser has, however, kept pace with the new trends and many flowering plants which a decade ago were suitable only for a large garden, may now be obtained in miniature form which makes them ideal for window boxes and small beds. As an example, whereas certain varieties of the beautiful godetia grow to a height of almost 2 ft. and in the exposed garden require staking, a new race of dwarf godetias are now obtainable and which form charming little rounded plants growing but 6–7 in. tall and being suitable for window boxes and the smallest beds. Within the next decade it is almost certain that most of our favourite annuals will be obtainable in miniature form.

These dainty plants may be used for the very smallest beds or for edging a bed of taller flowering plants in the larger garden. For all too long, those plants which through the years have been favourites for edging, for example, the lobelia and ageratum, have remained entirely neglected for providing the main bedding display in the small garden. It is as though the plants were suitable only for edging and yet a small bed planted entirely with varieties of either the lobelia or ageratum will provide a carpet of such rich colouring that should be seen to be believed possible.

In my own wind-swept garden, where the plants have also to endure the spray from the North Sea, it has been those of the most dwarf and compact form which have provided the most colourful displays during the adverse summers of 1956–7. Here, the dwarf annuals are not only used in beds to themselves, but are also used together, planting in circles or in strips, each to a single variety or colour, those plants of slightly taller habit being planted at the centre. In this way, beds may be planted with the Tom Thumb antirrhinums, the most dwarf of the ageratums, Sutton's dwarf godetias, the new miniature African marigolds and many more, to give brilliance of colour from early summer until the end of autumn.

The plants are equally attractive used to form small beds about a garden or around a courtyard where raised beds will provide the plants with the setting whereby they may reveal their maximum beauty. Along a path, or beneath the wall of a house they may be used, massed together to provide long strips of colour and planted about crazy paving stones. Nor is it necessary for a window box to be placed directly in front of a window. Boxes suitable for growing annual plants may be fixed around the walls of a courtyard where there is no garden whatsoever, or they may be used on a veranda or terrace, again where there is no bed of soil. The owner of a windswept garden, even where of large proportions, could well make use of these modern dwarf annuals instead of the more familiar taller growing forms.

Raising the Plants

Hardy annuals may be sown where they are to bloom, provided the soil is friable and well drained and especially is this essential where the seed is to be sown in early autumn, the plants being given biennial treatment to enable them to come early into bloom the following summer. The Tom Thumb antirrhinums, really of perennial habit but almost always treated as annuals, the Little Sweetheart sweet peas; and violas raised from seed and which are also perennial, may be raised under glass in a cold greenhouse or frame, or in boxes in the open, sowing the seed in July and transplanting into boxes in early autumn where the plants remain until set out in April. They will come into bloom fully a month before those plants raised in heat or where seed is sown in the open ground in spring.

A number of annuals, e.g. the godetia, linaria, viscaria and eschscholtzia, should only be sown where they are to bloom for they resent transplanting. Seed is sown as soon as soil conditions permit and this will be determined by the situation of one's garden. In the more favourable districts sow mid-March, in the northerly districts do not sow until the end of April. Nor is it advisable to obtain these plants from a nurseryman, for they are not likely to bloom well when transplanted however well they have been raised.

Where sowing in the open ground, do not sow the seed too deeply nor too thickly, and as soon as the seedlings are large enough to handle they should be thinned to 4 in. apart. Do not overdo the thinning for it must be remembered that the miniature varieties do not require as much room in which to develop as those of more vigorous habit and small beds should give as much colour as possible.

It is perhaps with the half-hardy annuals that most progress has been made in recent years in obtaining dwarf varieties. I am thinking of the petunia, the French marigold, *Phlox Drummondii* and nemesia, there being a number of introductions which for their compact habit, freedom of flowering and brilliance of colour could not have been contemplated in pre-war days. There is now a magnificent range of these half-hardy annuals, especially suitable for window box culture. Being half-hardy they should not be set out until the end of May or early June by which time the display of spring flowering plants or bulbs will have ended.

Half-hardy plants should be raised in gentle heat in the less favourable districts or in a frame where warmth from the early spring sunshine may be enjoyed. The seed should be sown in boxes or pans, the John Innes Sowing Compost being suitable. This may be obtained from a sundriesman or nursery already mixed to the following formula:

2 parts loam, preferably sterilized 1 part coarse sand 1 part peat $1\frac{1}{2}$ oz. of superphosphate of lime $\frac{3}{4}$ oz. of ground limestone	per bushel

The compost should be comfortably moist and friable at sowing time and should be kept in this condition whilst the seed germinates. Though the compost should never dry out, excessive watering will cause the tiny seedlings to damp off.

A temperature of around 50° F. will prove suitable and germination should take place within a month. If the seed is covered with brown paper to hasten germination and to prevent the compost from drying out too quickly, it must be removed the moment the seed has started to germinate. Also to prevent them becoming "drawn" it is important that the seedlings are transplanted to boxes containing a loamy soil, to which a little peat and sand has been added, as soon as they can be handled. The young plants should be kept growing on in a temperature of between 45° F.–50° F. until the end of April when they should be removed to a cold frame. Or they should be placed outside the greenhouse during the daytime so that by the end of May, they will have become well hardened and be ready for planting out.

Where it is not possible to raise one's own plants, purchase from a grower with a reputation to uphold and one famed for his well-grown plants. Plants which have been raised in too high a temperature and which are "drawn" and have not been hardened, will never give a good account of themselves however well the beds have been prepared. Where living within reach of a nursery, pay a visit during the Christmas holiday period, before the nurseryman makes up his seed order and state your requirements for the coming summer. Many nurserymen still do not cater for the very small gardener, whilst it is not possible to grow every variety of dwarf plants however worthy they may be.

Care should be taken in choosing suitable colours for plants together. A tiny bed of the Cupid African marigold edged with sky-blue lobelia, Blue Stone will give an attractive display. Or plant about the centre of a small circular bed the Dwarf Orange nemesia growing 8 in. tall, and surround with ageratum, Little Blue Star, which bears its fluffy mauve-blue flowers at a height of only 4 in. They will remain in bloom from the end of June until the end of October and will of course require no staking. Miniature flower beds should be slightly raised so that the full beauty of the plants is revealed.

Besides being inexpensive, annuals permit the ground to be kept thoroughly clean, the beds being cleared at the end of October and re-planted with spring flowering plants. This will also enable a small garden to be colourful from March until the end of autumn, fully eight months of the year. Only those plants should be used which will give a prolonged display of bloom and the choice should fall on those best able to withstand sunless periods and prolonged periods of rain. The choice is now considerable and in the following list of plants only those growing to a height of 9 in. or less will be described.

Dwarf Annuals for Summer Bedding

(H. = Hardy; H.H. = Half-Hardy.)

AGERATUM (H.H.). There are a number of new and most valuable varieties of this excellent window box plant, each of them being of compact habit and growing to a height of about 6 in. Little Blue Star, with its fluffy, navy-blue flowers; Capri, mid-blue; and the lavender, Blue Bedder, are all excellent. The new Swanley Blue covers itself with azure flowers and is just as compact. As an alternative to the blue ageratums, the pure white Little Dorrit is a most attractive form and is of similar height.

ALYSSUM (H.). With its close, prostrate habit and its blooms which smell of newly-mown hay, this is a most valuable plant for edging and for filling small beds. Or planted 8 in. apart over a raised, circular bed, the plants will form a mound of colour. Striking is the new Royal Carpet, with its blooms of bright royal purple. It is brighter and of more compact habit that Lilac Queen. Of the white varieties, Carpet of Snow is easily the best.

ANAGALLIS (H.H.). *A. grandiflora coerulea* is a pretty little plant for growing amongst crazy paving stone, for sowing along a path, or as an edging to a small shrubbery or flower bed. The large gentian-blue flowers are freely produced on neat plants. Sow where it is to bloom.

ANTIRRHINUM (H.). For massing in small beds, no summer flowering plant is more colourful, the Tom Thumb varieties and Carter's Dwarf Large-flowered strain growing to a height of only 7–8 in., whilst the Magic Carpet strain, ideal for a rockery attains a height of only 3–4 in. and forms a plant as wide as a dinner plate.

Of Carter's Dwarf strain, plants may be obtained in separate colours of apricot, scarlet, yellow, pink and white, the combinations of scarlet and yellow or scarlet and white presenting a striking display. Of the Tom Thumbs, the new Pinkie is quite outstanding; indeed, with its dainty spikes of strawberry-pink and cream it is one of the loveliest dwarf plants in cultivation. Others are Yellow Prince and Crimson King. The Magic Carpet strain is obtainable in a wide range of mixed colours.

ASTER (H.H.). It is the new dwarf wilt-resisting aster from the continent, Waldersee, which grows to a height of 9 in. which is suitable for bedding, window box or tub culture. The little busy plants cover themselves with dainty button-shaped blooms in shades of rose, scarlet, blue and purple. The plants remain in bloom until mid-October when they may be lifted and potted and in a cool greenhouse or room will continue to bloom until Christmas.

BRACHYCOMBE (H.H.). Known as the Swan River Daisy, this native of Australia enjoys a light, dry soil and a sunny position. It attains a height of only 9 in. and bears its blue, purple and lavender blooms from mid-June until October. Sow early in May and thin to 6 in. *B. iberidifolia*, Blue Star hybrids, is the best strain.

CANDYTUFT (H.). Sown where they are to bloom. Sutton's Dwarf hybrids grow to a height of only 6–7 in. and bear masses of flat blooms throughout summer, in carmine, lilac, purple and white.

COCKSCOMB (H.H.). *Celosia cristata* is its name and it requires a temperature of 60° F. in which to germinate the seed and bring on the quite tender plants which should be grown in pots and planted out early June. The best strain is Sutton's Prize Dwarf, the vivid gold and scarlet "combs" borne on only 6-in. stems. They will remain in bloom until cut down by frost at the end of October.

CORNFLOWER (H.). *Centaurea cyanus* is its correct name and the Dwarf Double flowered varieties of which Jubilee Gem, vivid blue, was the first to appear some twenty years ago, grow to a height of around 8 in. and remain long in bloom. Other varieties are Lilac Lady and Rose Gem, forming bushy little plants covered in small double flowers, whilst the new Polka Dot bears tiny double blooms in all the well known cornflower colours.

COTULA barbata (H.H.). This is quite a new plant to Britain. It is a native of South Africa and bears its rounded yellow rayless flowers from mid-July until late autumn. It forms a compact plant 4–5 in. tall and transplants readily.

DIANTHUS (H.). The annual dianthus has been improved out of all recognition in recent years and outstanding is the Persian Carpet strain which grows only 6 in. tall, making a spreading mat of dark green foliage which is studded with tiny pinks throughout the summer months. Used in small beds, or to edge a path this is an admirable plant, bearing blooms in shades of warm rose-pink, salmon, crimson and scarlet. It is best treated as a biennial, sowing seed in a warm room or greenhouse, in July and keeping the young plants in an airy frame until ready to go out in spring. They begin to bloom in June.

ESCHSCHOLTZIA (H.). Particularly valuable for poor, sandy soil and a position of full sun where seed is sown where the plants are to bloom. The dainty Miniature Primrose with its soft primrose-yellow blooms and growing to a height of only 5 in. is a charming plant.

FELICIA (H.). *F. geriana*, with its sky-blue star-like flowers borne on 6-in. stems is a plant deserving of greater popularity. Like all South African plants, it should be given a sunny position and dry soil. In bloom from June until October it makes a most valuable and original edging plant.

GAMOLEPSIS (H.H.). In its habit and bloom almost identical to the tagetes, bearing tiny golden flowers over the same long period and at a height of 8 in. Treat in the same way as for the ordinary tagetes.

GODETIA (H.). A dwarf flowering strain raised by Messrs. Sutton & Son, obtainable in lavender, mauve and salmon-pink and growing to a height of 6–7 in. now brings this colourful plant into the miniature garden category. Small beds, massed with the plants which have been sown where they are to bloom will present a brilliant picture. Not quite so dwarf, but growing to a height of no more than 9 in. is the new strain raised by Messrs. Hurst & Son of which Georgeous, velvet-crimson; Salmon Princess, salmon-orange; and Vivid, cherry and white are most striking.

LINARIA (H). The flowers of *L. Maroccana*, Fairy Bouquet, are like miniature antirrhinums, produced in profusion on 7-in. stems throughout mid-summer. The colour range is enormous, white, ruby, rose, purple, yellow, the spikes being neat and compact. Sow in any soil towards the end of March, no thinning being necessary if the seed is sown thinly.

LOBELIA (H.H.). Though, like the antirrhinum, strictly a perennial, the lobelia is always given annual treatment, the seed being sown in heat in February, covering the seed only lightly with sand and covering the box or pan with a sheet of clean glass to hasten germination. Whilst being hardened, it is advisable to pinch back those shoots which tend to become straggly to encourage a bushy plant. Most attractive beds may be made up by using lobelia of two or more varieties or with the dwarf Cupid marigolds. Or the plants may be used for edging or window box display.

Though the navy-blue, Mrs. Clibran, with its striking white eye, is the most widely planted of all lobelias, the paler Blue Stone is far more attractive planted with pink flowering plants, whilst the dark sea-blue Crystal Palace; the white Snowball; and the uncommon crimson-red Prima Donna, are all worth using by way of originality. Three or four varieties may be planted alternately to produce a colourful effect.

MARIGOLD (H.H.). It is not the Pot Marigold, the calendula, but the dwarf French and African varieties which are suitable plants for the miniature garden and window box. Though coming rather later into bloom than most annuals, they continue until November when they may be lifted and potted and will bloom indoors until Christmas.

Though most of the African varieties are tall growing, the new Cupid, which bears large yellow heads amidst fern-like foliage, grows only 6 in. tall and makes a bushy plant. The French marigolds may now be obtained with the most arresting markings of mahogany and gold, the markings being quite unique amongst flowers. In the double-flowered section, Gold Laced, the golden flowers having an attractive edging of carmine-red; Harmony, rich orange, with the outer petals deep mahogany; and Rusty Red, the crimson petals being edged with orange, are outstanding and rarely exceed a height of 12 in. In the single-flowered, Naughty Marietta, a tiny compact plant, the golden blooms blotched and striped maroon is most unusual, and the semi-double Bolero is attractive in mahogany-red with gold markings.

The pleasing use of concrete "stone" in a small garden

A garden of miniature roses. The plants grow 6–8 in. tall

Miniature Rose. Humpty Dumpty

MESEMBRYANTHEMUM (H.H.). These dwarf-growing succulent plants, native of South Africa, should be given a sunny position and a dry, sandy soil. They will survive almost desert-like conditions, remaining in bloom throughout summer and autumn, the daisy-shaped flowers opening only when the sun shines on them. *M. criniflorum* is also known as the Livingstone daisy, and no annual has a more brilliant colour range with its blooms of crimson, pink, apricot and yellow and numerous art shades.

MIMULUS (H.). Though perennial this is given annual treatment. Unwins' Choice Mixed strain grows only 6in. tall and bears flowers of yellow and red, spotted and blotched with black.

NASTURTIUM (H.). The dwarf single or Tom Thumb nasturtium just comes within the range of miniature plants. For a poor soil, it is an invaluable plant. From a March sowing where it is to bloom, the plants come into bloom in June and remain colourful until November. Outstanding varieties are Empress of India with its dark bronzy-green foliage and crimson-red flowers and Salmon Baby with dark green foliage and flowers of salmon-cerise held well above the foliage. They grow about 8 in. tall.

NEMESIA (H.H.). Like the marigolds, the modern nemesia has been improved out of all recognition during recent years, the habit now being more compact, more free flowering and remaining longer in bloom. Though classed as being half-hardy they are almost hardy, and like the marigolds are ideal for a northern garden.

One of the best strains is Hurst's Triumph Monarch which grows only 8 in. tall and bears flowers in every known colour including blue. Of named varieties, Fire King is scarlet; Orange Prince is glowing orange; and Blue Gem is sky-blue.

NICOTIANA (H.H.). The new variety Idol which grows only 9 in. tall, bears bright scarlet flowers and which begins to bloom in early July, several weeks before other nicotianas, and remains colourful until the frosts. Making a wide bushy plant, the flowers are untroubled by wet weather.

Sow seed in gentle heat early in the year and grow on the seedlings in peat blocks or small pots, hardening before planting out late in May.

PETUNIA (H.H.). This is one of the more tender bedding plants, requiring to be raised in heat and planted out in early June. With their ruffled trumpets of the most intense colouring, great freedom of flowering and compact habit, petunias provide an unequalled display.

The seed should be sown with care early in the year in a greenhouse heated to 65° F. Seedlings should be pricked out into individual pots. Established plants like plenty of moisture at the roots and frequent syringing will keep the foliage free of aphis.

The F.1. hybrid petunias, with their intense richness of colouring are too vigorous for the miniature garden. Instead Sutton's Dwarf Compact strain should be used; the bushy little plants grow no more than 8 in. high and cover themselves in brilliantly coloured trumpets in rose, scarlet, purple, mauve and white. Another lovely strain is the Giant Victorious Double which grows 8 in. tall, its globular flowers being almost like pin cushions with their density of petal, and measuring 3–4 in. across. They are obtainable in all the well known petunia colours, including purple and white, and crimson and white striped.

PHACELIA (H.). Producing its pinnacles of Hair-bell-like flowers of a rich mid-blue, on 9-in. stems and coming into bloom early in June from an early April sowing, *P. Campanularia* is one of the most colourful of all edging plants for a dry, sandy soil. Thin to 4 in.

PHLOX DRUMMONDII (H.H.). For long this charming and colourful annual phlox spoilt itself by its straggling habit, the stems requiring to be pegged down as growth advanced. No longer is this necessary for Carter's Globe strain and the American Twinkle strain both possess a compact, upright habit, growing only 7–8 in. tall and remaining in bloom throughout summer and autumn. They are most charming plants for a tiny bed or for a window box, Carter's strain bearing a globe-shaped head and obtainable in the glorious pastel shades of mauve, salmon, buff, apricot, pink and cream as well as the more brilliant crimsons; whilst the Twinkle strain bears an attractive star-like flower in a similar colour range.

PORTULACA grandiflora (H.). This native of South America is quite hardy in this country and is a charming carpeting plant of almost prostrate habit. It is called the Sun Rose for it likes a sunny position and a dry soil of a poorish nature where from July until October it will bear masses of cup-shaped flowers in yellow, rose, purple, orange and white. There is also a double form known as Thompson & Morgan's Improved strain, the blooms resembling carnations, the colours of orange, scarlet, rose and white being noted for their intensity and clarity. They are held on only 3 in. stems.

PYRETHRUM parthenium (H.). Few know it by its botanical name for it is Featherfew, the species *P. aureus* having bright golden foliage, the new variety Golden Moss making a rounded plant only 5 in. tall. It is a colourful plant either for the centre display of a small bed or for edging and though really perennial it is always given annual or biennial treatment like the antirrhinum. The seed is sown in July in boxes covered with glass or in a frame. As soon as they can be handled, the seedlings are transplanted to boxes where they remain in a frame or cold greenhouse until May when they are planted out with the other summer bedding plants.

SPECULARIA (H.). Venus's Looking Glass, as *S. Speculum* is called, is a delightful edging plant, from an early April sowing flowering from mid-July until September on 9-in. stems. The deep violet bell-shaped flowers sow themselves as readily as forget-me-nots and quickly come into bloom.

SWEET PEA (H.). The introduction of the Little Sweetheart race of this ever-popular plant, making compact, rounded bushes 6–8 in. high and the same distance wide, has brought about its use for bedding. The plants may be sown in early autumn, in a cold frame in March or in gentle heat and planted out early May. The plants should be set out 9 in. apart and will require no staking.

SWEET WILLIAM (H.). Sow in June and treated as a biennial, or in spring in ground where it is to bloom. The Wee Willie strain which grows less than 6 in. tall remains long in bloom and bears clusters of red, white, salmon and rose coloured flowers, also with many delightful bi-colour combinations.

TAGETES (H.H.). *T. signata pumila* Golden Gem, with its feathery foliage and brilliant yellow star-like flowers is a member of the same family as both the French and African marigolds. It grows to a height of 8–9 in. and though for long widely used for edging, it is perhaps more attractive planted in beds with blue lobelias with which it forms a pleasing contrast. The variety Lulu is a canary-yelow counterpart of Golden Gem, and Hurst's Lemon Monarch is clear lemon yellow.

VERBENA (H.H.). This delightful bedding plant is yet another of those tender perennials which is always given half-hardy treatment. In the north there is a tendency for the plants to come rather too late into bloom, being at their best during late August and through September. In the south the plants, from a February sowing in heat, come into bloom at the end of July. Amongst the best varieties are the pure white, Crystal, and the scarlet Sparkle. They are of compact, upright habit, the shoots requiring no pegging down. The plants enjoy a position of full sun, but do like a moist soil.

VIRGINIA STOCK (H.). Growing to a height of 5-6 in. and obtainable in shades of crimson, mauve, white and blue, these dainty little plants are delightful for edging a border, sown at the end of March. No thinning is necessary if sown thinly.

ZINNIA H.H.). The first true bedding strain of this arresting Mexican flower is Thumbelina, the plants growing only 6 in. tall and bearing their rubbery-petalled flowers in vivid colours of orange, red, pink and yellow from mid-July until the frosts.

Chapter 4

DWARF PLANTS FOR SUMMER BEDDING

Exotic plants for summer bedding – Begonia – Fuchsia – Gazania – Geranium – Pentstemon – Pink – Rose – Salvia – Viola.

In addition to the many suitable annuals of compact habit, there are many lovely perennial plants to provide a brilliant display in the very small garden during the months of summer and autumn. These plants, which include the begonia and salvia and members of the geranium family, as well as a number of interesting plants having colourful foliage, are amongst the most valuable plants of the garden and will provide colour over a period of at least twenty weeks, for a longer period than will any other plants. Nor is it necessary to own a greenhouse to enjoy their beauty though most may be classed as being somewhat tender in our climate and so the plants will require lifting and storing in a frost free room after flowering. This will enable the beds to be cleaned and planted during early November with miniature bulbs or with spring flowering plants and these will in turn be replaced after flowering with the summer flowering plants early in June or towards the end of May in the south. The plants are excellent for small outdoor beds, also for window boxes and tubs which are possibly grouped around a tiny courtyard. Against a whitewashed wall, the brilliance of the bloom or foliage will be difficult to equal by that of any other plants.

BEGONIA. The charming multiflora begonias which make small, bushy, rounded plants and grow only 5–6 in. tall are wonderful plants for a tiny bed or for a small window box. They may, in fact, be used anywhere about a small garden, massed together in troughs or boxes to provide five months of vivid colour. No plant has a more compact habit, nor is more colourful for its size, having glossy bronze-green foliage and covering itself in a mass of tiny blooms. But perhaps the great value of this plant is that it will continue to bloom in profusion in spite of the weather, weeks of continuous rain and wind having little effect on the display. The begonia being a lover of a damp soil should always be grown on the western side of Britain, with the geranium and its preference for dry conditions on the eastern side. The begonia is a native of the moist, humid climate of South America, the geranium of South Africa with its dry heat.

The multiflora begonias are tuberous rooted and so may be started into growth in a box of peaty soil in the sunny window of a warm room. This is more satisfactory than planting out unstarted tubers, for they take six weeks to form shoots and this time should not be wasted by planting dormant tubers directly into outdoor beds. Also, there will be less likelihood of the young shoots being severed by slugs where started in boxes. A warm greenhouse will prove equally suitable, though it is not a necessity and few can afford to use artificial heat apart from the natural warmth of the sun. The tubers may be started in a closed frame, though they will be rather later to make growth.

The beginning of April is the best time to plant the tubers, which cost about 10s. 6d. a dozen, and a dozen will fill a bed approximately 3 ft. × 2 ft. or a circular bed of a diameter of 4 ft. It should also be remembered that though the outlay will be greater than where annuals are used, the tubers, given care in their storing will remain healthy for many years and may readily be increased by dividing the tubers, as they grow large, into pieces containing an "eye" which will produce a shoot. Boxes containing a 2-in. depth of compost should be used, about 70 per cent moist peat making up the compost, together with a little sandy loam. The surface should be made level and firm, the tubers being merely pressed into the compost leaving the flat portion exposed. From here the shoots will sprout if the compost is kept comfortably moist and a buoyant atmosphere is maintained. From the beginning the tubers must always be kept moist.

By mid-May, the tubers will have formed several leafy shoots and will be ready for hardening before planting out. This may be done by placing the plants outdoors on all suitable occasions and lifting them under cover at night until fear of frost has departed, when the plants may be set out. They may also be started in 3-in. pots, one tuber to each pot. This will ensure an early display for they will receive no check on being planted out. Tuberous begonias, however, generally transplant easily and will soon come into bloom and make bushy plants provided they do not lack moisture. Their liking for moisture is made clear during a wet summer when the plants bear an abundance of bloom.

The soil for begonias should contain plenty of humus in the form of decayed manure, used hops, leaf mould or peat and especially is this necessary where the soil is light and sandy. Plant 9 in. apart and make comfortably firm though taking care not to break the fleshy shoots when moving the plants. Should the weather continue dry, which it so often does during June, place peat to a depth of half an inch around the plants and water as frequently as necessary.

The plants will continue to bloom until the first hard frost, though the beds may be required for bulbs or spring flowering plants by the end of October when the begonias should be carefully lifted, foliage included, and placed in an airy room to die back gradually. The stems should then be removed and the tubers stored in boxes of dry peat in a frost free room until restarted into growth in April. To propagate, cut the tubers into two or three pieces with a sharp knife as soon as it is possible to determine the eyes or shoots. The cut portions should be rubbed in sulphur to prevent decay and should be planted in small pots to grow on. The plants may be grown entirely in pots, transferring to a 60 size pot in which they are to bloom.

Possibly the finest variety is Jewel, the blooms measuring nearly 2 in. across and being of a luminous apricot-orange colour, enhanced by its dark bottle-green foliage. The leaves are pointed, with serrated edges. Extremely colourful is Flamboyant, the blooms being vivid scarlet, the foliage rich green; whilst Mrs. Richard Galle bears a bloom of buff-apricot. Helen Harms, with its two-tone colouring of yellow and orange is outstanding, also the new Madelon with its blooms of deep pure pink.

There is another dainty small flowered begonia suitable for window box and tub culture and for the smallest beds and which is known as *B. gracilis*. It makes a plant of upright habit, about 9 in. tall and has beautiful, glossy leaves, the tiny blooms being borne in clusters. The plants have the same freedom of flowering and ability to withstand adverse weather as the multifloras but being fibrous rooted require a warm greenhouse for their culture. Seed sown in a sandy compost in the early New Year in a temperature of between 55° F.–60° F. will make plants which will bloom outdoors in July and continue until autumn. If potted, they will continue to bloom in a warm room throughout the winter. Those who have no form of heat may obtain plants from specialist growers ready for planting out about June 1st. Costing no more than 6s. 6d. a dozen, they may be treated as annuals and destroyed after flowering.

One of the most richly coloured of all plants is *B. gracilis*, Indian Maid, the foliage being chocolate-bronze, the flowers crimson-red; whilst Prima Donna has beautiful glossy green foliage and bears a bloom of deep carmine-pink. Both grow 9 in. tall, but for the very small bed the new Saga 1, growing only 4 in. tall and bearing a bloom of crimson-red, and Karin, with its snow-white blooms and dark green leaves, provide a contrast when planted together which is difficult to better.

FUCHSIA. The shrubby little fuchsias make remarkably attractive summer bedding plants and are not as widely planted as they should be. With their pendulous blooms they are most graceful and make little rounded bushes no more than 8 in. tall, whereas most bedding fuchsias grow to a height of 20 in. or more. The two best varieties are Tom Thumb, which bears rose and purple flowers and Lottie Hobbie, even more dwarf and which bears crimson-red flowers with attractive long stamens.

The plants are quite happy in partial shade and they like a soil enriched with a little decayed manure and which is well drained in winter. Propagation is by cuttings rooted round the side of pots towards the end of summer as for salvias and pentstemons. The plants should be set out in May, planting firmly and about 8 in. apart.

GAZANIA. It is *G. splendens* with a variegated leaf and large daisy-like bloom of brilliant orange which is the most valuable for bedding. Where the plants are set out in a small bed 8 in. apart in May, they will quickly carpet the whole bed so that no soil is to be seen, whilst the semi-prostrate plants will be a mass of colour until lifted towards the end of autumn. This is a half-hardy plant, the plants being wintered in a warm greenhouse. Propagation is by cuttings rooted in a sandy compost in early autumn. As soon as rooted, the plants should be potted into 3-in. pots where they are kept quite dry and are grown on in a warm greenhouse or room. The plants should be hardened before being planted out in May or early June.

GERANIUM. Though more widely grown than any other summer bedding plant, most of those used in this way are too robust for a very small garden though most geraniums may be considered to be of reasonably compact habit. There are, however, in all sections a number of plants of dwarf habit which makes them very suitable for a miniature garden and for small window-box culture. It is in the ornamental leaf section that most of the dwarf varieties are to be found and in the very wet summers of the past two or three years, there is much to be said for their use to the exclusion of those which are generally grown for their bloom. It should be said that geraniums do not withstand adverse weather so well as the multiflora begonias, and to have them in bloom to best advantage, they do like a dry soil and a prolonged period of dry weather. For this reason they are more satisfactory planted down the drier eastern half of Britain where, given a sunny season they will bloom profusely for weeks on end with no more attention than the removal of dead blooms and foliage.

The plants like a soil enriched with a little decayed manure, preferably cow manure, worked deeply into the soil but otherwise they require no other form of humus and are never happy where peat is used. They are ideal plants for a sun-baked situation where they should be grown to the exclusion of all other plants. The plants are set out towards the end of May, but being pot grown and able to withstand the generally dry conditions of June, they may be planted out at any time during that month.

A delightful small bed may be made up by planting at the centre the charming silver-leaved, Chelsea Gem, which bears double flowers of fuchsia-pink and surrounding it with the old French variety, Mephistopheles with its bronzy-black foliage and tiny vermilion flowers. Like Black Vesuvius, which it resembles in all respects, though its foliage is possibly a shade darker, it grows only 5–6 in. tall.

A new variety of great beauty is Nero. Growing only 6 in. tall, the leaves are almost black, the stems and blooms being fiery-red. The leaves have an interesting scarlet flush at the centre. This variety could be edged with the effective silver-leaved Mrs. Salleron, which does not bear flowers, but has most striking foliage. Or use the tiny Tom Thumb, which has vivid green zoneless leaves and tiny bright rose-pink flowers, attractively tipped with white and is most inexpensive.

Other attractive miniatures are Claudius, having bottle-green foliage and bearing a white bloom veined with rose; Kleine Liebling, having vivid green leaves and pink flowers; and that old favourite Golden Harry Hieover, which has a golden leaf with a bronze zone and bears scarlet flowers. Those who favour the large, richly coloured blooms of the Zonal geraniums and where the size of garden permits their use, will find Lady Sarah Wilson most free flowering and extremely compact. The bloom is of an unusual combination of white, edged with red. Two others of extremely compact habit are Duchess, which bears a semi-double bloom of a lovely shade of phlox-pink; and Mrs. Lawrence, which bears a double bloom of carmine-red. These are lovely plants for a window box or tub, edged with one of the dark-leaved miniatures and are more compact than the familiar Paul Crampel.

Several of the charming scented-leaf varieties have a compact habit, particularly Fair Helen, the daintiest of the oak-leaf varieties, the small leaves being extremely pungent, the tiny blooms having the appearance of orchid-purple moths. Equally dainty is Prince of Orange, the small, bright green leaves releasing a rich perfume of oranges when pressed. Also of compact, bushy habit is *G. fragrans*, the velvety green foliage releasing a strong pine fragrance. And where a dwarf trailing variety is required for a garden ornament or sunny corner, the ivy-leaved Mrs. Martin is just right, its fully double blooms being the exact colour of a violet chocolate cream. The charming miniature pelargoniums, not suitable for bedding, make ideal pot plants as indeed do all members of the geranium family, those mentioned being most suitable for the small room. The plants may be grown entirely in pots or maybe lifted from outdoor beds or window boxes and grown on in 60 size pots in a frost-free room throughout the winter when any unduly long shoots should be pinched back before planting out again in summer. Where only small numbers of plants have been grown, this is the best way to winter them, keeping the roots as dry as possible. Geraniums do require a frost-free room and failing the provision of a warm greenhouse or room in the home, the plants should be lifted and placed in boxes with their roots covered in dry soil. They should be removed to a shed or attic room to winter. It will be advisable to cut back the shoots and to remove all foliage, giving the plants a dusting with sulphur to prevent mildew. If kept dry and and clear of frost the plants will have every chance of surviving the winter.

To propagate, remove the cuttings during summer and insert round the sides of a pot filled with sandy soil. When the shoots have rooted, re-pot into individual 3-in. pots and grow on during winter in a frost-free room or warm greenhouse, planting out in June.

Delightful additions to the range of geraniums are the true miniature Regal or Show pelargoniums. They are quite distinct from the dwarf zonal varieties with their colourful foliage and which bear little bloom, for they are famed for the beauty of their flowers as much as for their foliage. The bloom is like that of the Show pelargonium but in miniature form, whilst it is produced without a break right through summer and early autumn; new blooms replacing those that drop their petals in one steady succession. They are also the first of the pelargonium family to come into bloom early in April indoors where they are perhaps happier than planted outside.

The plants rarely exceed a height of 9 in., remaining bushy and compact and never becoming straggling as do many of the Shows. They are charming plants for a small room, being constantly in bloom and requiring almost no attention the whole year round other than an occasional watering during summer. Neither gas nor central heating seems to trouble them in any way. Outdoors they are better able to withstand adverse weather than the large flowered Show varieties and so are valuable for a window box or for planting in small beds.

Cuttings may be taken and struck during August and September. The cuttings root more readily than most pelargoniums, for the shoots are short jointed and quite "hard". Three or four should be inserted round 3-in. pots and kept comfortably moist when they will root in three weeks. Nothing could be easier. Potted into individual pots early in October they should be kept almost dry through winter, then given more water to bring them on in March. For a potting compost, use a fresh fibrous loam to which is added a small amount of sharp sand, and some very well decayed manure which all pelargoniums love.

As soon as the newly-rooted cuttings begin to grow in spring, it is advisable to pinch out the growing point when it will be found that new shoots will appear from soil level, making a most compact plant. They may be planted outside early in June, or they may be grown on in a greenhouse, or a sunny window of the home where they will remain healthy and free flowering for years.

A most attractive variety is Catford Belle, with its large orchid-mauve flowers, blotched petunia-purple, its foliage being pleasantly rose-scented.

A new race of these hybrids known as the Langley Smith Miniature Pelargoniums, which have bloom like tiny azaleas and beautifully marked, includes Mr. H. G. Smith, white, with attractive mauve upper petals; Newcourt, pale mauve, veined rich purple; Kerlander, soft shell-pink; Langley, salmon-pink, flushed purple; and Spring Park, lavender-mauve. There is also one having scented foliage and beautiful cyclamen flowers, called Floris. Others of interest and charm are Petit Pierre, of perfect miniature form and bearing a bloom of rich Tyrian rose; and Sancho Panza, with its bloom of rich purple. A delightful little plant is Tom Thumb, which has pale green zoneless leaves and rose-pink flowers tipped with white.

Another new race introduced for the first time in 1957, have striking black-green foliage and have all been named after Roman Emperors. They are as yet expensive, but extremely beautiful, forming compact little bushes only 6–8 in. in height and are extremely colourful whether in bloom or not. Striking with its white blooms and almost black foliage is Claudius; whilst Nero bears not only striking vermilion-red flowers but its bronzy-black leaves have a distinct red flush, the plants being as if on fire.

With their ease of propagation and culture, long flowering period and the fact that the plants are ideal for the smallest of rooms, as many as a dozen being accommodated on a window ledge, or in a small window box must surely bring these delightful miniature pelargoniums great popularity in future. They are also quite inexpensive, costing between 3s. 6d.–5s. each, and if kept in a frost-free room over winter will last for years, retaining the fresh bright green colour of their foliage.

A new strain of F.1 hybrids which grow only 9 in. tall may readily be raised from seed sown in gentle heat in the new year and planted out in June, come up into bloom in August. They may be moved to small pots in October to continue the display through winter in a temperature of only 50° F. Or sow in April; the plants will begin to bloom under glass in September. The salmon and scarlet shades are most colourful whilst the new variety, Sprinter, bearing large but compact heads of crimson-red, is most striking and can be used either for bedding or as a pot plant.

PENTSTEMON. Though often treated as half-hardy, plants raised from cuttings being wintered in a warm greenhouse and planted out in May after being hardened, the pentstemon is quite hardy and in most districts will winter outside quite unharmed. Though several species bloom only during the months of May and June, one or two of dwarf habit remain in bloom from June until October, forming compact little shrublike bushes growing only 6–8 in. tall and proving ideal bedding plants. They may be treated as perennial, which they are, and carpeted with double daisies or the most dwarf of the primroses such as F. Ashby and Snow Cushion so that the bed will give colour from March until October for the minimum of trouble. *P. pinifolius* makes a charming plant having pine-like foliage and bearing tiny spikes of scarlet trumpets; whilst *P. heterophyllus*, True Blue, slightly taller growing, bears spikes of sky-blue trumpets above grey-green foliage.

The plants like a well-drained soil but do not necessarily require full sun. A sandy soil, well drained in winter and in which a little decayed manure is incorporated, suits them well. Propagation is best from cuttings, rooted round the sides of a small pot and wintered in a cold frame or greenhouse.

PINK. Whilst the Border carnation is too tall growing for the miniature garden and the old-fashioned pink has only a short flowering season, the Allwoodii pinks with their compact habit and long season of flowering make excellent plants for summer bedding and what is more, they are perennial and extremely hardy. The most compact grow only from 6–8 in. tall and with their bushy habit and attractive silver-grey foliage they will be ideal for bedding, planted 9 in. apart, or used to edge a path or border. For tubs, window boxes and on the rockery, they are most suitable. The blooms, about the size of half a crown are held above the upright foliage on rigid 6-in. stems and unlike the old pinks, they do not burst their calyx.

Pinks will only grow well where the soil is well drained for they are never happy where the roots are troubled by excess winter moisture. They also require a soil containing plenty of lime though no manure. Established plants will benefit from a dressing of hydrated lime given in October each year. Pinks also demand a position of full sunlight and never flourish in shade. Given the conditions they enjoy, the plants will remain compact and free flowering for several years, any unduly long shoots being removed each year after flowering.

Propagation is by means of cuttings or pipings taken from shoots which have not flowered. Inserted in a compost of peat and sand in frames or around the side of a pot, rooting will take place in three weeks. The plants may be grown on in 3-in. pots or may be allowed to remain in the frame until spring when they are planted out. Do not plant too deeply or the main stem will decay. Make quite firm and apart from the removal of dead bloom, the plants will require no further attention.

Of those varieties of dwarf habit, Robin, bearing double blooms of scarlet-orange; Victor, maroon and rose, also double; and Freda, mauve-pink are plants of great beauty. Also excellent is the Allwoodii hybrid, Yellowhammer, the first yellow pink with double blooms. The Alpine Allwoodii, also valuable for a trough garden and rockery, may also be used for bedding. Amongst the best for this purpose is Mercury, with its semi-double bloom of cherry-red; Tinkerbell, shell-pink; Jupiter, salmon-pink; and Dewdrop, white with an attractive green eye.

ROSE. See Chapter 2.

SALVIA. One of the most colourful and compact plants for a miniature garden is the new salvia, Scarlet Pigmy, which forms a bushy little plant only 6 in. tall and the same distance in width. Planted out in small beds surrounded by white alyssum or the silver leaf miniature geranium, Madame Salleron, the bed will remain colourful throughout summer and autumn. The salvias will bloom more freely if the dead flower stems are cut out as they form; others will quickly take their place.

Though easily raised from seed in a temperature of 65° F., an expensive way in these days of high fuel costs, salvias are best propagated from cuttings taken towards the end of summer. The cuttings which should be about 3 in. long, are inserted in boxes or around the rim of a pot in exactly the same way as geraniums, or the bedding plants may be lifted in late October, transferred to pots or boxes, and if kept in gentle heat, will continue to bear cuttings during winter. These may be removed and rooted in batches as they form. They should be kept in a temperature of 55° F., syringing them frequently to guard against red spider. As soon as rooted they are transferred to 3-in. pots. The salvia is a gross feeder and must be given a compost containing a stiff fibrous loam, decayed manure, a little grit to keep the compost "open", and a small quantity of bone meal. To keep the habit compact, the plants should be firmly potted. They should be transferred to cold frames for hardening about mid-May and given copious amounts of water. The plants should also never lack moisture when planted out and they like a soil well enriched with humus in the form of peat and manure.

VIOLA. For a small garden, no plant will provide a colourful display over so long a period as will the bedding violas, but care must be taken to select only those having a compact and free flowering habit. A large number of the named violas are exhibition plants, the bloom being almost as large as those of the mammoth flowering pansies and the habit of the plant similar. And whilst they bear a large bloom, they are not sufficiently free flowering to be used for bedding. It is those of *V. gracilis* type which should be planted, the blooms being about the size of a two shilling piece and borne with profusion on 4-in. stems well above the foliage. Of the named varieties, possibly the best for bedding is Bluestone which bears a mass of bloom from April until early November without the plant ever becoming straggly. The blooms are a beautiful mid-blue and have an attractive golden eye. Of similar habit is Palmer's White; whilst the old variety Bullion, bears its small yellow flowers in similar profusion. Another free flowering variety is Jackanapes, the upper petals being crimson-brown, the lower petals bright yellow, whilst Maggie Mott with its silvery-mauve blooms is also extremely free.

Propagation of these named varieties is only by cuttings. These should be taken during August and September from unflowered shoots and inserted in frames or boxes of sandy soil to which a small amount of peat is added to retain moisture. The plants will be ready for planting out the following March or early April and in a soil which does not lack humus will remain vigorous for two or three years.

Beds may be made up of several varieties and may be interplanted with double daisies to give colour in spring, or miniature bulbs may be used. The plants are most attractive used to edge a bed of dwarf roses.

Of those varieties which may be expected to come true from seed, Chantryland with its golden flowers, flushed with apricot and orange; C. H. Kay, purple-blue with a striking yellow eye; and the new Campanula Blue, lovely pale blue, have a dainty, compact habit and are extremely free flowering. Another strain of dainty, compact habit is *V. cornuta*, Bambini growing only 5 in. tall, the flowers resembling violettas in their appearance and obtainable in subtle tones of pastel pink, apricot, red, lavender and bronze. This is an ideal plant for edging or for rock gardens.

Seed should be sown in drills outdoors or in boxes of John Innes Sowing Compost in July, the seedlings being transplanted as soon as large enough to handle. Through summer and autumn they will build up into sturdy plants to be planted out in October or March when they come into bloom early in summer.

Equally attractive are the charming Violettas, their dainty oval blooms being held on 4-in. stems and dancing in the breezes. Lovely for a rockery, for edging and for planting in tiny beds they are of more perennial habit than all other members of the viola family and are extremely free flowering. They are best increased by division of the roots as soon as new growth commences in spring, the smallest "pieces" quickly growing into a strong clump. With their ease in propagation, they may be recommended to those who have neither the means nor the time to take cuttings or sow seed.

The blooms are entirely rayless, the original Violetta, from which the race takes its name, being still obtainable, the blooms being of a lovely creamy white shade. Perfection bears bloom of clear sky-blue, whilst Mrs. Grimshaw bears bloom of a pleasing shade of rose-pink. Others of charm are Dawn, primrose-yellow; Le Grandeur, mid-blue; Heather Bell, mauve-pink, and Little David, cream. Most possess a delicate violet fragrance.

Chapter 5

SPRING FLOWERS

The adaptability of spring flowering plants – Auricula – Double daisy – Erysimum – Myosotis – Pansy – Primrose – Polyanthus – Violet – Wallflower.

QUITE apart from the attractive miniature bulbs, there are many lovely plants which bloom during the springtime to make colourful the smallest of gardens as well as window boxes and tubs. With the blooms appearing during winter and spring, a number even bearing their bloom beneath a covering of snow, no plants are more appreciated, their bloom being so eagerly awaited following the dull, cold days of winter. No garden should be without at least a few of these charming plants, for by their compact habit they are happy in the very smallest of gardens. The miniature polyanthuses and primroses may be used in a shady corner, likewise the dwarf forget-me-nots, the winter flowering pansies and the violets, whilst the dainty double daisies and a number of the primulas may be used to advantage in the trough garden. All are suitable for a window box and for use in the small tub. Indeed, they are the neatest of all plants. They are extremely hardy, most of them being just as happy in an exposed northerly garden as they will be in the most sheltered garden of the south. By their dwarf, compact habit they are untroubled by strong winds, whilst periods of frost seem only to accentuate their freedom of flowering and the rich colouring of their bloom when it appears. Remaining in bloom from the first days of spring until early June, when the summer flowering plants take over, they should be used about the garden as lavishly as possible, together with the miniature bulbs to make their contribution in providing an all-year-round display of colour.

AURICULA. The lovely old Border auriculas are ideal plants for a very small garden for they have a more compact habit than even the primrose and are tolerant of intense cold and town conditions. To edge a small path or a small shrubbery, for planting in tubs or ornamental vases, or in beds to themselves, they are amongst the most colourful plants with their richly coloured bloom and mealy grey-green foliage. The plants should be set out into a soil enriched with humus and once planted should be disturbed as little as possible. The plants will, however, benefit greatly from a dressing of peat or leaf mould given each year after flowering has ended in early June, for the plants tend to form their new roots almost at soil level. A mulch will also help to maintain moisture in the soil during summer.

The named varieties are increased by root division, the plants being lifted every three or four years, whilst an inexpensive method is to raise plants from seed. This should be sown under glass in April, a box covered with a sheet of clean glass will be satisfactory, the plants being transferred to small pots or boxes when large enough to handle. The plants will be set out in their flowering quarters in October.

Of the named varieties Adam Lord has a most compact habit, the navy-blue flowers with their white centre being held on sturdy 5-in. stems. Of similar habit is Broadwell Gold, which bears a large golden-yellow bloom with a strong fragrance, the petals being attractively waved whilst both bloom and foliage are covered in meal. Of extremely rich colouring is Craig Nordie, bearing large burgundy-red blooms and having silvery foliage; whilst Queen Alexandra bears a pale primrose-yellow bloom which is powerfully fragrant. Very dainty in habit is the brilliantly coloured Southport, the orange-scarlet blooms held on 4-in. stems; whilst Linnet, equally compact bears a bloom of green, brown and mustard colourings, the colours of the linnet. The famous old Dusty Miller auriculas are more suitable for the larger garden.

CHEIRANTHUS. Known as the Siberian Wallflower, it possesses extreme hardiness and is easier to grow than the ordinary wallflower. It forms a rosette-like plant which has grey-green leaves and bears its densely packed sprays of orange-yellow at a height of about 12 in. Seed may be sown in July where it is to bloom, or in shallow drills and the plants transplanted into their flowering quarters in March or April. It comes into bloom late in spring, several weeks after the ordinary wallflower and remains colourful until towards the end of summer when the plants are usually dug up and destroyed.

Golden Bedder is a long established variety of known brilliance, but of recent introduction is Apricot Delight, its flowers being of a lovely shade of apricot-orange.

DOUBLE DAISY. The most suitable varieties for a miniature garden or for planting as a ground cover for bulbs are not the large-flowered types such as Snowball and the red-quilled Etna which tend to grow rather coarse, but the dainty Rob Roy, crimson; Dresden China, shell-pink; and The Pearl, white, which bear fully double button-like blooms on 3-in. stems. They are most charming plants, never becoming coarse and remaining long in bloom. They are propagated by root division, the offsets being planted into beds

The dainty miniature Pelargonium, Catford Belle

Primula Garryarde Guinevere

New French Marigold, Rusty Red

New dwarf African Marigold, Golden Crown

immediately after flowering. They should be set out in their flowering quarters in autumn, planting them 4–5 in. apart. They are delightful planted about a rockery in groups of three or four or around a tub. They may also be used in a trough garden, in a window box and as an edging to a small bed. Charming in this way is The Pearl, used to edge a bed of primrose, Betty Green with its brilliant scarlet blooms. Or plant a circular bed of the compact primrose Snow Cushion with Rob Roy daisy, the combination of crimson and white being most attractive.

ERYSIMUM. For winter and spring colour planted in small beds, in window boxes, at the front of a shrubbery, or on a rockery *E. achroleucum*, Golden Gem will be perpetually in bloom from October until May. It is a member of the cheiranthus family and is known as the Alpine Wallflower. It is like a miniature cheiranthus in habit and in the shape and colour of its bloom. It makes a compact, tufty plant and is well able to withstand severe winter weather. Plant 6 in. apart and in a soil which is well drained, or in a slightly raised bed. Seed should be sown in early April in drills in the open and if the seedlings are thinned early, transplanting may not be necessary, the plants being set out in October.

MYOSOTIS. Indispensable plants for a shady bed, for planting with bulbs to form a ground cover, or for massing in beds with yellow wallflowers, the forget-me-not is one of the most useful plants of the garden. In the large garden, the tall flowering varieties may be used and these are allowed to seed themselves, for it is rarely necessary to keep them within bounds. The hybridist has, however, raised a number of new varieties most suitable for a tiny garden or window box. They make charming little plants or bushes 6 in. tall and of similar width and remain covered in bloom for weeks on end. One of the best varieties is Monarch Blue Ball, which bears a large bloom of deepest indigo. Excellent too is Carter's Azure Beauty, the bloom being of a lovely shade of pale, smoky-blue; whilst Star of Love bears a bloom of mid-blue.

Seed should be sown in a shaded bed outdoors during the early weeks of June. If the seed is thinly sown, transplanting may not be necessary, for the myosotis is of easy culture and makes a bushy, fibrous-rooted plant without much help. Plant out in October 6-in. apart, a little closer together where growing in a window box.

PANSY. All pansies and violas raised from seed sown the previous July or August will come into bloom the following spring though some will bloom earlier than others, whilst the winter flowering strain and the new Clear Chrystals strain obtainable for the first time in 1958, will bloom throughout a mild winter and will be a mass of bloom from early April onwards. If a second sowing is made in gentle heat or under a frame early in March, the plants will be in all their glory during the latter weeks of summer and throughout autumn, when the earlier flowering varieties will be coming to an end.

Though pansies and violas raised from seed may be left to bloom a second year, their culture is so easy and the seed so inexpensive that to enable the beds to be cleaned and to enjoy greater freedom of blooming, they are best treated either as annual or biennial plants, a sowing being made in July and another in early March.

No plant is more useful about a garden than the pansy and viola and for the small garden those of compact habit, bearing a small, neat bloom should be grown. They are happy in partial shade and just as satisfactory in a town garden as in the country. If they have a preference it is for the cooler regions, though where grown in the south or in a position of full sun they should be given a soil well enriched with humus. This may be in the form of a little decayed manure, leaf mould, used hops or peat. Only where the plants do not lack summer moisture will they continue to bloom over a very long period, almost for twelve months.

Seed is sown either in a frame or in the open ground towards the end of July or early August. Where growing only a few plants, seed should be sown in boxes or pans containing the John Innes Sowing Compost, just covering the seed. It should be kept moist or germination will be delayed. As soon as the seedlings are large enough to handle they should be transplanted either to boxes or to a small open ground bed, where the plants grow on until October when they are transferred to their flowering quarters, setting out the plants 6 in. apart.

Where space and labour are at a premium, inter-planting is to be recommended and where the Clear Chrystals strain is used, the plants may be set out between bulbs or dwarf polyanthuses and primroses. If the bed is planted in late October, the plants will come into bloom during the first warm days of spring and will remain colourful until the end of autumn. If small pots of bulbs such as crocus Imperati are inserted in the bed with the pot rim just covered, they will come into bloom early in the New Year and if the hardy polyanthus Barrowby Gem, with its yellowish-green almond-scented blooms is also used there will be rich colour throughout the latter part of winter, through spring and early summer, when the pansies come into their full beauty. Where the true winter flowering pansies are grown, they will come into bloom early in winter from a July sowing and continue through periods of inclement weather from that time until the latter weeks of summer.

To prolong the display, all dead bloom should be removed as it forms, so that the plant does not use its energies in setting seed. A little peat, pressed around the crown of the plants during early summer will do much to retain moisture in the soil and keep the roots cool.

Of the winter flowering pansies, the dark velvet-blue March Beauty and the golden Helios are attractive planted together; also the pure white Snowstorm planted with Wine Red. Others of beauty are Blue Boy with its blooms of silvery-lilac; Winter Sun, yellow with a dark eye; and Orion, bearing a large golden bloom.

Others of compact habit are the Felix pansies, the immensely rich blooms of bronze, fawn, purple and crimson shades having pronounced black "whiskers". Excellent too, is the Peter Pan strain in mixed colours and particularly attractive are the pure china-blue flowers of the first named variety, Porcelain Blue. The glorious Swiss Giants and strains such as Engelmann's Giant are better for the larger bed, but of more compact habit is Harrison's Syston strain, the small blooms having the familiar pansy blotch and a remarkably fine colour range, whilst blooms of the Clear Chrystals strain consist of the most beautiful self colours and are without any blotch or markings giving them a brightness equalled by few other pansies.

PRIMROSE. This plant is amongst the most useful for the small garden and whilst almost all the primrose varieties may be classed as having a compact habit, some are more suitable for the very small garden than others. Indeed whereas the lovely new variety, Perle von Bottrop which bears a vivid royal purple bloom, makes a quite substantial plant, having foliage of upright habit, a number of the Juliae primroses are of almost prostrate habit and bear their bloom on short 2-in. stems above the foliage. Such varieties are ideal for troughs, for edging tiny beds of miniature bulbs, and for planting in shaded beds entirely to themselves. They are also excellent carpeting plants for bulbs. Extremely hardy and tolerant of the soot-laden atmosphere of a town garden, these dwarf primroses will quickly form a clump as large as a dinner plate. Propagation is by dividing the roots after flowering or in autumn, the smallest pieces making a good-sized plant within twelve months.

Un-named varieties may be raised, and they will provide rich colour for at least ten weeks, from seed sown in spring in boxes in the open covered with glass or in a cold frame. They will have formed good-sized plants by October and will bloom in spring. The plants may be left untouched in their flowering quarters for at least a second season, when they should be lifted and divided.

All members of the primrose family appreciate partial shade and so may be planted around the roots of orchard or ornamental trees, one or so enhancing most gardens, however small. The plants will also prove colourful in beds or corners to which the sun does not penetrate and where few other plants would flourish.

Late autumn is the best time for planting and a soil enriched with humus to retain summer moisture will be necessary. A plant which has not sufficient moisture at the roots will not only make little new growth but will have only a short life. Humus should be provided in the form of hop manure, seaweed, decayed farmyard manure, peat or leaf mould.

To provide colour during the earliest days of spring, the polyanthus-primrose Barrowby Gem, which carries a delightful perfume should be grown. Its yellowish-green flowers are held on sturdy 6-in. stems and it will bloom from the early New Year until early June. Another of similar type and in bloom over the same period is the new Hunter's Moon, its bloom being best described as luminous apricot and possessing as powerful a fragrance as Ena Harkness rose. But of those of most compact habit for a very small garden, the dainty Keith bearing lemon-yellow blooms on 4-in. stems, like a miniature polyanthus, is most attractive. Others include E. R. Janes, with its blooms of salmon-orange; Snow Cushion, its clear white blooms held above the most dainty foliage on 1-in. stems; F. Ashby, with its tiny crimson blooms and with attractive crimson stems and foliage; Bridget, its clear mauve-pink blooms appearing late; Garryarde Victory, with its paeony-purple blooms and bronzy-green foliage; and Dinah, its velvet-crimson blooms having an attractive olive-green centre. Two others of extremely neat habit and producing their dainty blooms on less than 2-in. stems are Pam, with its crimson-purple blooms, and Tiny Tim, a cherry-red counterpart and having vivid green leaves.

The lovely double primroses are mostly of neat habit, possibly more so than the single Juliae primroses but are rather less robust. Enchanting is Red Paddy, with its dainty button-like blooms of orange-red, laced with silver. Equally neat is Bon Accord Lilac, the lilac-pink blooms having an attractive orange centre. Another for the tiny bed is Chevithorne Pink, its dainty rounded blooms of lovely orchid-pink being held in polyanthus fashion on 3-in. stems. Others are Our Pat with its blooms of amethyst-blue and bronzy foliage; Cloth of Gold, pale yellow; Arthur du Moulin, deep violet-purple; and Quaker's Bonnet, known to Elizabethan gardeners, the bloom being of delicate clear mauve.

Of the hose-in-hose primroses, one bloom growing inside another, there is a tiny form of Pam, whilst Lady Mollie bears a bloom of bright rosy-mauve. Most charming too is Lady Lettice, the cream and apricot flowers held on 4-in. stems, dancing in the breezes.

POLYANTHUS. Of similar habit to the primrose and requiring exactly the same culture, it may be said that all the polyanthus strains are suitable for the small garden, though for the very small garden the miniatures are even more suitable. There are several lovely named varieties and a new strain which comes true to type from seed. This has been evolved by the Barnhaven Gardens of Oregon, U.S.A., the extremely dainty blooms being held on 4-in. stems. Of the named varieties, Lady Greer, with its neat, rounded foliage and blooms of pale moonlight-yellow borne on 5-6 in. stems is a charming plant, ideal for edging, or for planting on a rockery or in a window box. Similar in habit is Dr. McWatt, the blooms being of a rich shade of purple-claret.

Of other strains, Sutton's Superb is most compact, bearing flowers embracing a wide colour range, and Hansen's hybrids are of outstanding quality and intensity of colour, the individual blooms being as large as an old crown piece. Blackmore and Langdon's Blue strain is compact and noted for its clarity of colour, a bed in full bloom being delightful when edged with the dainty pink double daisy Dresden China.

Nor must the old Gold Laced polyanthus be left out of the spring display, for the blooms are most striking with their band of almost black with adjoining circles of gold leaf colouring.

The Gold Laced polyanthus is of neat habit, the crimson blooms, some almost black, being beautifully edged with gold. Of the ordinary bedding strains, one of the most compact is Sutton's Superb, embracing a wide colour range. Blackmore & Longdon's Pink and their Blue strain are also of compact habit, making them ideal for window boxes and small beds. They are delightful edged with double daisy, Dresden China.

VIOLET. Unlike the primrose family, though the violet enjoys similar conditions of dappled shade and a soil well enriched with humus, it is never happy in the polluted atmosphere of a town garden. Clean air is essential to healthy plant life and only in seaside or country gardens does the violet flourish. Though widely grown in the south-west for its early bloom, this does not infer that it is in any way tender. Indeed the violet is amongst the hardiest of plants and is to be found on the hills of Lanarkshire as it is about the hedgerows of Sussex. Like all members of the viola family the violet makes a sturdier plant where growing under cool conditions, where it bears a bloom of much finer quality. It will, however, be quite happy in shade, and dappled shade suits it most of all. Like all members of the family the plants like a soil which retains summer moisture, so incorporate as much humus as possible.

As the plants reproduce themselves from runners, they are best when planted in a bed to themselves where their runners do not interfere with other plants. They may also be increased by division of the crowns, early May being the most suitable time. Rooted runners may be detached as they form and have rooted. As the "strings" which join the rosettes will also form roots, a small piece should be severed with the rosette. This will ensure the plants getting away to a good start in their new bed. Plant 6 in. apart and throughout summer any runners or bloom which may form should be removed, so that the plants can concentrate their entire energy on the production of bloom the following spring. Throughout summer, the plants should never be allowed to lack moisture.

To enjoy very early bloom, one or two plants may be covered with a cloche but a sunny position should be selected for those plants expected to bloom early.

After the plants have finished flowering and the runners have been removed, the old crowns should be dressed with either peat or decayed manure so that they will bloom well the following year, after which they should be divided and replanted into a new bed.

There are some very beautifully coloured violets quite apart from those bearing a bloom of typical violet colouring and a few plants of each should find a place in the smallest of gardens. One of the best of all is Admiral Avellan, an extremely hardy variety bearing a bloom of bright reddish-purple and possessing a strong perfume. Equally hardy, though not having so strong a fragrance is the new Bournemouth Gem, the blooms being of a deep purple-blue colour. A variety which is strangely neglected is Coeur d'Alsace, which bears its sweetly perfumed rose-pink blooms on long stems. Owing to its resistance to pest and disease, the scentless Governor Herrick which will bloom well in a shallow soil, has become popular. Its blooms are of a bright purple colour. One of the loveliest is the little known John Raddenbury, which bears sweetly perfumed blooms of bright china-blue. Most attractive too, is Irish Elegance, which bears a bloom of creamy-buff and one of the most beautiful of all is Countess of Shaftesbury, the lavender-blue flowers having a centre row of petals of rose-pink and green stamens. The double flowering varieties are less hardy than the singles and suitable only for southern gardens.

WALLFLOWER. Everybody's favourites on account of their richly coloured and fragrant blooms, only a small number of the many wallflower varieties may be considered suitable for the smallest of gardens. Nowhere are the plants more appreciated than where planted close to a doorway or window, where their rich perfume may drift into the house during the calmer days of spring. For the unduly exposed garden wallflowers, unless so well grown that they will have attained bush-like proportions at planting time, may suffer from frosts and cold winds, whereas the primrose and polyanthus would be untroubled by such conditions and should be grown where extreme hardiness is desired.

To grow wallflowers really well, they should be given a long season and the end of April is not too early to sow the seed. Use seed saved the previous summer so that it is fresh and will germinate quickly and sow in drills 6 in. apart or broadcast in a small seed bed thoroughly cleaned of weeds and to which some peat has been added. Sow thinly, raking in the seed lightly and keeping moist. To prevent any woody tap root from forming, the old gardeners would transplant three or four times during summer over a slate bed, but equally good wallflowers may be grown if the young plants are moved to a bed of prepared ground as soon as large enough to handle, spacing them 4 in. apart. All too often the plants are allowed to remain in their seed bed far too long, until they have become "drawn" and weakly, from which condition they may never recover. Where ground is at a premium, seed may be sown in deep boxes and the plants moved to boxes containing 6–8 in. of soil. The plants will be set out into beds towards the end of October and they like a deeply dug, fairly rich soil and firm planting.

The most suitable for small beds and for tubs and window boxes will be Messrs. Sutton's special Dwarf Bedding strain, the plants growing no more than 8 in. tall and include all shades of yellow, brown, rose and crimson. Also suitable will be Orange, Primrose, Scarlet and Golden Bedder, each growing to a height of only 9 in. Planted in strips or circles of individual colours the effect will be extremely rich from April until early June. Plant 6–7 in. apart.

Chapter 6

HARDY BORDER PLANTS OF DWARF HABIT

The modern border plant – Preparation of the soil – Planting – Back row plants – Mid-border plants – Front row plants.

As with other plants, the hybridist has, during the past decade, concentrated on introducing hardy border plants suited to modern conditions. The small garden has demanded a plant of compact habit, which will be in proportion to its surroundings whilst shortage of labour for the garden has meant that all plants should be as labour saving as possible. Those massive herbaceous borders to be found in most spacious gardens at the beginning of the twentieth century and which demanded considerable time and expense in the staking and tying of the plants most of which grew from 4–7 ft. tall, are now rarely to be seen. Instead, the plants must be of most compact habit, generally no more than 4 ft. in height and capable of blooming over a long period with the minimum of attention. The plants too, should be of very perennial habits those which tend to die back after two or three years finding little favour.

The compact, upright habit of the modern border plant makes it possible to plant a herbaceous border in the smallest of gardens, using plants which grow no more than just over 3 ft. tall. Three rows of plants should be used planting those between 9–18 in. in height at the front, those between 1½–2½ ft. tall in the centre; with those plants around 3 ft. tall at the back. The length of the border will depend upon the ground at one's disposal, but the width should be no more than 3 ft., less than half that of the herbaceous borders of old. This will permit the back row plants to be attended without treading the ground. Such a border, made up of plants of neat compact habit will enable a herbaceous border to be made in the most exposed garden, whilst these same plants may even be used for bedding in the larger garden. It will be necessary to select those plants which bloom over a long period owing to the restricted size of the border and so that there will be revealed the maximum of colour at one time. By careful selection of the plants it will be possible for the border to be colourful from May until almost the end of November, when the plants should be cut back to 6 in. of their base and the ground forked between them. If at the same time it is enriched with a little decayed manure, used hops or some peat, the border should not require disturbance for at least four years. Today there is a wide range of plants suitable for all soil types, also for shade.

Preparation of the Soil

Much may also be done to bring various soils into a condition in which most border perennials will flourish and first, where the border is to be made in a town garden, where the soil is generally of an acid nature caused by deposits of soot and sulphur, it should be given a good dressing with lime as the ground is prepared. If the soil is sticky and contains a high proportion of clay particles, it will be desirable to break up the particles so that the soil will be better aerated and drained and there will be less likelihood of the plants decaying, due to excess moisture collecting about the roots during winter. Unhydrated or caustic lime should therefore be incorporated as the soil is being dug over to a depth of at least 15 in. The action of moisture on the lime will cause it to disintegrate, at the same time breaking up the soil.

The work should be done early in autumn, the ground being cleared of all perennial weeds at the same time. Early in November some humus should be incorporated and almost any humus forming materials will be suitable, such as decayed garden refuse, well-rotted manure, seaweed, peat and used hops which are generally obtainable from a local brewery. If it is not possible to obtain any manure, fork in some peat and give a dressing with bone meal, 2 oz. per square yard. It will be advisable to allow the ground ten days in which to settle down before planting so that there will be no air pockets about the roots after planting. It should be said that a light, sandy soil will require more humus than will a heavy soil to enable it to retain moisture during dry summer periods. Hardy border plants are copious drinkers and heavy feeders and if they are to have a long life and bloom over an extended period they must never lack moisture at their roots.

Planting

Where the soil is light and friable, planting is best done during the third week of November for if delayed until spring, such a soil may suffer from lack of moisture, dry periods often being experienced during spring and early summer, thus making it difficult for the plants to become established. Where the soil is heavy and not too well drained, planting will best be delayed until the end of March. From autumn planting, however, a much better display of bloom may be expected the first summer than if planting is delayed until spring.

The plants are best set out in groups of three so that there will be a liberal splash of colour from each variety. Odd plants set here and there about a border will never make a pleasing display, nor where the plants conform to formal planting. Ample space should be allowed between each group rather than between each plant, though the plants should be set out in groups according to their vigour and habit. It is also important to arrange the colours to provide pleasing contrasts, planting those which bear a yellow or orange flower near those bearing a blue or purple bloom. Pink also contrasts well with blue, likewise red with white. And whilst it is desirable to use those plants having as long a period of flowering as possible, not all will reach their full beauty at the same time and so care must be taken to see that there are no ugly gaps about the border, which will be devoid of colour for long periods. Near those plants which come early into bloom, the lupins and delphiniums of dwarf habit, plant those which bloom late in the season, the heleniums and perennial asters. Then in front of these plant the lupins and monarda which also bloom earlier in summer. Near the May-flowering doronicum plant the August flowering phlox. About the border plant several groups of those very long flowering plants such as the *Achillea Eupatorium* and *Poterium obtusum*, with its attractive pink blooms like bottle brushes. Before ordering the plants and before any planting is done, the border should be carefully planned, selecting long flowering plants of compact habit which require the minimum of attention. Set out the plants when the soil is friable and quite free of frost, make them quite firm, then rake over the ground between the plants. As a guide to planting, rings of sand may be made on the surface of the soil and small labels placed in each on which has been written the name of the plant, colour of the bloom and flowering time, following the plan previously made on paper. This will permit the plants to be set out without delay, to the correct distance apart and exactly as planned.

Back Row Plants for a Small Border 3 ft.

ACHILLEA Eupatorium. With its beautifully "cut" silver-grey foliage, strongly aromatic, and bearing its flat heads of brilliant yellow from July until late October on 3-ft. stems, this is a magnificent border plant. Coronation Gold and Flowers of Sulphur, both well named are outstanding new varieties. Plant near the michaelmas daisies at 18 in. apart. Two plants together will make a fine display.

ANCHUSA italica. The old varieties grew to a height of 5 ft., but the new Loddon Royalist, which bears masses of bright blue flowers from June until early September reaches a height of no more than 3 ft. Plant, as for most blue flowering plants, in early spring. The new Little John, with its deep flowers, grows only 15 in. tall.

ANEMONE japonica. In bloom from early August until November, this is a lovely plant for growing near the michaelmas daisies and like them it enjoys a moist soil. Max Vogel, with its semi-double blooms of clear pink; Louise Uhink, pure white; and Herzblut, rose-red, each bloom at a height of just under 3 ft. Plant 18 in. apart. Bressingham Glow bears crimson flowers on only 18 in. stems.

ASTER. No border will be complete without the liberal use of the michaelmas daisy, members of the *novae-belgii* group flowering from early September until mid-November. Plant them with the rudbeckias, 15 in. apart and use those flowering on 3-ft. stems to the back of the border. Of those varieties which bear blue flowers, Ada Ballard, F. M. Simpson, Marie Ballard and The Sexton bear very large blooms on 3-ft. stems. In pink shades, the new brightly coloured Tudor Rose; Orchid Pink, with its attractive golden centre; Lassie and Charmwood are amongst the best. In crimson shades, Crimson Brocade; Winston Churchill, beetroot-red; The Rector, claret-red and Red Sunset are outstanding. As a contrast, Chorister is a lovely pure white and in purple-violet colours Flying Enterprise with its plum-purple flowers; Festival, orchid-purple, and Petunia, violet are amongst the best.

For mid-border planting or for the back row of a very small border are several of the finest of all michaelmas daisies including Fontaine, with its large tawny-pink bloom with an orange centre; Tapestry, double rose-pink; Violet Lady, deepest purple; Winsom Winnie, rose-red; Melbourne Belle, crimson-red; and Chequers, violet-mauve. All grow to a height of a little over 2 ft.

ASTILBE arendsii. For a moist, peaty soil these are valuable plants and if several varieties are planted together, bloom may be enjoyed from early July until mid-September. Plant one each of three or four varieties in a group. Erica, with its feathery spikes of clear pink is the first to bloom; followed by Fire, with its plumes of salmon-red. Then comes Dusseldorf, bright salmon and lastly, Jo Orphorst, which bears its ruby-red spikes well into September.

COREOPSIS. In bloom from early June until September, this is a most colourful plant and like *Doronicum*, the blooms last well in water. The attractive flat blooms are borne on 3-ft. stems and Badengold, pure golden-yellow is most showy. Excellent too is Astolat Variety, the golden blooms having a crimson blotch. Plant 18 in. apart. Goldfink bears deep yellow flowers on only 12-in. stems.

DELPHINIUM. It is the dainty Bella Donna hybrids that are suitable for a very small border for they bloom at a height of only 3 ft. They possess a far more feathery habit than the tall large-flowered varieties and make a charming display during June and July. Planting should take place in March, about 20 in. apart. Orion, medium blue and Capri, with its sky-blue flowers are extremely compact, also the new white, Elstead White. Plant with it Wendy, with its blooms of gentian-blue or *D. ruysii*, Pink Sensation, with its spikes of delicate salmon-pink.

DORONICUM. So valuable in that it comes into bloom before the end of April, bearing its large yellow daisy-like flowers above pale green foliage and is quite happy in partial shade. Very compact and free flowering is Miss Mason, orange-yellow; whilst Bunch of Gold, with its canary-yellow flowers is slightly later to bloom and is of similar habit. Plant 18 in. apart.

HELENIUM. Most of them come into bloom in July and remain colourful until late autumn, their daisy-like blooms, with their attractive dark cone centres being borne in large sprays. Many are too tall growing, but several of the newer varieties may be ideal plants for the small border. The old Crimson Beauty, with its crimson-brown flowers and growing to a height of only 2½ ft. is excellent for the middle of the border, likewise July Sun, its large golden flowers being flushed with orange, whilst Wyndley bears a bloom of similar colour and has the same habit. Excellent is the new Goldlackzwerg which bears blooms of gold, flecked with crimson on 3-ft. stems, whilst Butterpat, late flowering, bears a bloom of butter-yellow.

KNIPHOFIA. No small border will be complete without these lovely old plants, generally known as Red Hot Pokers, though now there are pure white and yellow flowering varieties. Yellow Hammer, bearing its spires of golden-yellow, in bloom from July until September, grows to a height of less than 3 ft., whilst Maid of Orleans, of similar habit bears spikes of pure ivory-white. Plant near them the compact and long flowering Lord Roberts, with its pokers of orange-flame. Planting should be done singly, allowing the plants 3 ft. in which to grow.

LUPIN. Though of sturdy habit, most of the lovely Russell lupins would be rather too vigorous for the small border. Several, however, bloom at a height of rather less than 3 ft. and amongst these is Rita, with its dainty spikes of deep crimson. Another is Mrs. Micklethwaite the bells being salmon-pink, the standards gold; whilst Mrs. Garnet Botfield, bears a compact spike of golden-yellow. Compact too is Flaming June, which bears a spike of orange-crimson, flushed with gold. Because of their bushy habit plant 2 ft. apart.

LYCHNIS chalcedonica. Flowering from June until early September on 3-ft. stems, this plant with its flat heads of flaming scarlet gives a splash of rich colour to any border. Plant 18 in. apart. There is a double flowering variety, *rubra plena,* which grows to a height of only 2 ft. and should be used at the middle of the border.

RUDBECKIA. A new series of dwarf varieties of this late summer and autumn flowering plant have taken the place of those which bloom on 6-ft. stems. Outstanding is Goldsturm and equally valuable is Goldquelle, both of which bear fully double blooms of golden-yellow on 3-ft. stems. The former blooms from early July until mid-September, the latter from early September until late in November, so plant two or three together for a succession of bloom.

SALVIA. With their attractive grey foliage, several of the salvia species are superb plants for the back of a small border. *S. nemorosa* bears its dainty spikes of violet-purple for a period of at least ten weeks on 3-ft. stems, whilst a dwarfer form, *compacta,* is a lovely mid-row plant. Likewise *S. haematodes,* which bears silvery-lilac blooms on branched stems from July until October. Plant 20 in. apart in spring.

SIDALCEA malvaeflora. With their marshmallow-like flowers in shades of pink, a number of the new sidalceas are of sufficiently compact habit for a small border. They prefer a sunny position and should be planted 18 in. apart. Revealing quite a new colour break is the compact William Smith, the blooms being large and of a warm shade of salmon-pink. A charming variety is Dainty, its shell-pink blooms having an attractive white centre. Very compact too, is Loveliness, which bears spikes of glowing pink.

SOLIDAGO. This, the Golden Rod has been greatly improved of recent years, the plants now being short and compact with their plumes of yellowish-green possessing more substance and remaining colourful over a much longer period. The plants will grow well in partial shade and in any soil. Growing to a height of less than 3 ft. is Golden Shower, with its arching sprays, whilst the earliest to bloom is Lineralis, with its plumes of bright yellow. Excellent for the front of a border is the new Queenie, which bears its dainty sprays on only 12–14 in. stems.

Mid-Border Plants $1\frac{1}{2}$–$2\frac{1}{2}$ ft.

AQUILEGIA. The new McKana Hybrids from America with their huge bi-coloured blooms and so easily raised from seed, will bring the Columbine a new popularity. The plants are especially happy in a shaded position.

CHRYSANTHEMUM. The Korean and Pompone members of this large family which grow to a height of no more than a little over

2 ft. are ideal mid-border plants and may be left undisturbed for several years. During early autumn they produce a more brilliant mass of colour than almost any other plant and are of course excellent for cutting. Plant in spring 18 in. apart. Outstanding for its large double orange blooms is Korean Carlene, whilst Polly Peachum bears a bloom of a lovely shade of peach-pink. Also of compact habit is Sunny Day, the canary-yellow blooms having a delicious perfume, while Tapestry Red bears a double crimson bloom. In the Pompone section, Bob covers itself with tiny buttons of vivid scarlet; Denise, with golden yellow blooms, Titania, with orange-bronze blooms; and Little Dorrit bears blooms of a delicate shade of shell-pink.

CHRYSANTHEMUM maximum. This is a fine, compact long flowering perennial, the varieties Esther Read and Jennifer Read bearing their fully double pure white blooms on 2-ft. stems throughout summer. The plants are happy in ordinary soil which must be well drained in winter. Plant 15 in. apart in groups of three.

ERIGERON. The modern varieties do not hang their heads like those of old, whilst the blooms are of richer colours. Growing to a height of about 20 in., the new Foerster's Liebling, bearing semi-double flowers of pure pink, and Dimity, which grows only 12 in. tall and covers itself with orange-pink flowers are excellent for the front of a border. Plant 12 in. apart in spring.

HEMEROCALLIS. Known as the Day Lily, for its richly coloured blooms last for only twenty-four hours before others take their place, this is a fine mid-border plant, the most dwarf varieties blooming on 2-ft. stems. Their dahlia-like tuberous roots are best planted in autumn, 18 in. apart in groups of two or three. Possibly the three best for a small border are Viscountess Byng, orange; Royal Sovereign, golden-yellow, and Radiant, orange-red.

INULA. With its compact habit, its grey-green foliage and large-rayed flowers of bright golden-yellow, this is a valuable but little known perennial. The blooms are born on upright 20-in. stems and remain colourful from June until early September. *I. Royleana*, bears striking orange-rayed flowers, whilst *I. oculis christi* bears bright yellow blooms of similar form.

LYSIMACHIA punctata. Bearing upright whorls of golden-yellow flowers on 2-ft. stems, with its compact habit this is an excellent plant where space is limited and it does well in any soil. Plant 18 in. apart. It blooms from mid-June until the end of August.

LYTHRUM. With their bushy habit and bearing masses of thin pencil spikes from July until September, this is a fine mid-border plant and possibly the two best varieties for a small garden are Robert and The Rocket, both of which bear spikes of pure rose-pink. The Beacon, with its crimson-red flowers is rather taller growing but could be used for the back of the border.

MONARDA. The Bergamots are excellent plants with their pungent foliage and upright flower stems and are happy in full sun or partial shade. Plant 15 in. apart in groups of three. The new Prairie Glow, bearing its salmon-red blooms on 2-ft. stems is very showy, whilst Adam, crimson and Cambridge Scarlet have a similar habit and richness of colour.

PAEONY. Most valuable plants for they are happy in partial shade and will remain vigorous for fifty years in a rich, humus laden soil. Plants, containing three "eyes" are best planted in October and November, the only time when they are really dormant. Plant 2 ft. apart and not too deeply. Certain varieties are taller growing than others, but of those that are reasonably dwarf are Duchess de Nemours (white) and Sarah Bernhardt (silvery-pink), the first to bloom, followed by Elizabeth Stone (satin-pink) and Peter Brand (crimson) and the shell-pink, Pure Delight one of the last to bloom. Each possesses a distinct fragrance.

PHLOX. The recent introductions, noted for their compact habit are also less troubled by eelworm than the older varieties. Whilst the lovely Symons-Jeune phloxes are rather too vigorous for the small border, the Regal phloxes are of compact habit. Sandringham, with its large trusses of cyclamen-purple; Glamis, rich pink; and Windsor, carmine-red, all bloom on 2½-ft. stems. The lovely new Blue Lagoon and the pure white Rembrandt, of similar habit, could also be planted in groups 12 in. apart. Other new varieties of outstanding beauty are San-Antonio, claret-red; Gaiety, salmon-orange; and the well named Look Again which bears huge trusses of glowing mulberry-purple.

POTERIUM obtusum. This so neglected plant is one of the longest flowering of all perennials; from June until November it bears its fluffy pink blooms like bottle brushes and is one of the loveliest of all plants. It grows to a height of 2½ ft. and should be planted 18 in. apart.

SCABIOUS. Lovers of lime, the scabious remains longer in bloom than most perennials, coming into bloom in midsummer and remaining colourful until almost the year end. The flat blooms, with their cushion centres are borne on 2-ft. stems which are almost leafless. Plant in spring, 20 in. apart. Still one of the best is Clive Greaves, with its large blooms of mauve-blue and great freedom of flowering. Also lovely is Imperial Purple, with its bloom of deepest purple, and Rosalind bearing bloom of a new shade of wistaria-blue.

TROLLIUS. Extremely valuable in the border in that it blooms very early in summer when there is little colour in the border. The globular flowers are borne on erect 2-ft. stems, the plants being set out 18 in. apart in groups of two or three. The three best varieties are possibly Alabaster, a new variety from Germany which bears ivory blooms; Salamander, fiery orange; and Canary Bird, primrose-yellow.

Front Row Plants 9–18 in.

A number of very charming junior editions of the more robust perennials may now be obtained and which are very suitable for making up miniature borders for the smallest of gardens.

ANAPHALIS triplinervis. Its broad silvery-grey foliage and compact heads of papery white flowers lends distinction to the front of a border. It is especially striking near the deep purple erigerons and salvias. It grows only 12in. tall.

ASTER. The dwarf forms of *A. novae belgii* are indispensable plants for autumn flowering, remaining colourful from early September until November making compact mounds of 9-12 in. tall. Little Blue Baby and Lilac Time do not grow more than 6 in. tall and are lovely for a small rockery. Other lovely varieties are Queen of Sheba, lilac-pink; Peter Pan, clear rose-pink; Midget, pale blue; Victor, light blue; and Little Red Boy.

CAMPANULA. The new variety, Pouffe is one of the few border campanulas to bloom over a long period. It forms a tiny mound 9 in. high and covers itself in masses of light blue flowers from June until early September. *C. glomerata dahurica* grows only 12 in. tall and forms a dense clump, its violet bell-shaped flowers appearing in clusters at the end of stiff stems.

DICENTRA. They are graceful shade-tolerant plants bearing their nodding heart-shaped flowers (the Bleeding Heart of cottage gardens) on arching sprays 12 in. long. The plants are enhanced by the much-divided blue-grey foliage. Bountiful is in bloom from May until September. *D. eximia alba* bears sprays of pure white flowers.

ERYNGIUM. An interesting plant is *E. varifolium* growing 16 in. tall and of stiff upright habit, its spiny blue flower heads surrounded by ivory bracts whilst its prickly leaves have striking white veins.

GERANIUM endressi. The variety Wargrave Pink is one of the longest flowering of all perennials, from June until November. It forms a bushy plant 15 in. tall and should be planted 2 ft. apart. It bears small cup-shaped blooms of a beautiful clear pink. A hybrid, Johnson's Blue of similar habit, bears bloom of clear blue. Plant one of each together.

GEUM. The two best varieties are the yellow flowered Georgensburg and Fire Opal with its intense flame coloured blooms. Both form compact little plants, flowering on 15-in. stems from the end of May until the end of August, almost twice as long as the other geums. Plant 9 in. apart.

HEUCHERA. Excellent plants for a dry, sandy soil the new hybrids bear their graceful clouds of bloom on arching stems 18 in. tall. Red Spangles, the best of all, bears sprays of deepest crimson, whilst Shere Variety bears vivid scarlet flowers. Plant with them Snowflakes with its pure white blooms.

HEUCHERELLA. A hybrid of the *Heuchera* and *Tiarella*. The variety Bridget Bloom is in flower from May until late in August, bearing its tapering spikes of tiny shell pink flowers on 15-in. stems. It does well in semi-shade.

INCARVILLEA delavayi. One of the loveliest plants of the border, it is tuberous rooted and has dark green pinnate leaves above which it bears, on 12-in. stems in June and July, large wax-like trumpets of rosy-mauve. Bees Pink bears shell-pink flowers.

OENOTHERA. This, the perennial form of the lovely Evening Primrose is a lovely plant, in bloom from mid-June until September. *O. fruticosa* Yellow River bears its large yellow cup-shaped blooms on 18-in. stems and is happiest in a sunny position.

ONOSMA echioides. It is generally thought to be rather too tall for a rockery and slightly too dwarf for the herbacious border, so it is rarely seen and we miss much for it is one of the loveliest plants of the garden. It likes a well-drained soil and a sunny situation, where from mid-June until later in August it bears its rich golden tubular flowers in pendulous form on 8–9-in. stems. The blooms also carry a delicious almond fragrance. It is, indeed, one of the loveliest of all plants and is extremely hardy.

PAPAVER orientale. For long the Oriental Poppies with their habit of falling along the ground if not well supported have been grown in borders, but for the tiny garden, plant the lovely Peter Pan of upright habit. The larger salmon-scarlet blooms are borne on 12-in. stems. Another bearing its bloom on erect stems 20 in. long is the double crimson-red flowering, Border Beauty.

PHYSOSTEGIA. The variety Vivid, bears its almost square spikes of shell-pink flowers on 12-in. stems and blooms from early July until September. Summer Snow bears pure white flowers.

PLATYCODON. This is an unusual and charming plant for a small border, bearing its balloon-like flowers of pale blue on 12-in. stems from July until September.

POLEMONIUM coeruleum. Jacob's Ladder of cottage gardens, so called because of its neat pinnate foliage and multitudes of tiny sky-blue flowers, colourful during May and June. The form Blue Pearl grows to only 9 in., half the height of the species.

POLYGONUM affine. A lovely plant, it bears spikes of crimson-red on 12-in. stems during August and September and during autumn the leaves turn an attractive golden colour.

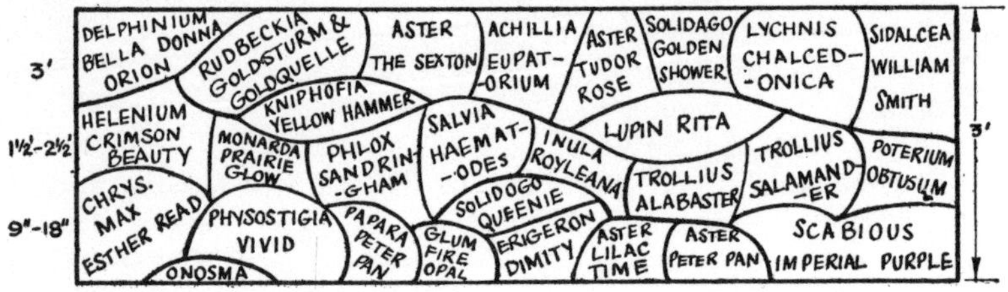

POTENTILLA. Like geums, the small rounded blooms remain colourful from June until September, being held on 12-in. stems. Gibson's Scarlet and the semi-double Yellow Queen are the most dwarf varieties.

PRUNELLA. Through June and July the variety Pink Loveliness bears its dainty spikes of clear pink flowers on 12-in. stems above attractive dark foliage. It likes a rich soil and a sunny position.

STACHYS lanata. Known as Donkey's Ears on account of its handsome, long, silvery-grey leaves, it is a most attractive plant bearing spikes of bright tubular pink flowers clustered together.

STOKESIA cyanaea. It is in bloom throughout late summer and early autumn, the large lavender-blue flowers borne on 12-in. stems. Plant 12 in. apart and in spring.

TRADESCANTIA. Quaint, in that the propeller-like flowers are backed by a long leaf, these natives of Virginia remain in bloom from June until late in August, bearing their bloom on 18-in. stems. J. C. Weguelin bears a bloom of pretty sky-blue; Osprey, a white bloom; whilst Gayborder Violet bears a bloom of deepest purple. Plant in groups of three or four, 9 in. apart.

VERONICA spicata. The new form, Minuet has glossy grey-green foliage and bears dainty spikes of pure pink from July until early September. It grows to a height of 15 in. and is a charming plant. To grow with it, use *V. teucrium* Shirley Blue, in bloom over a longer period, the vivid mid-blue spikes growing only 12–14 in. tall.

Chapter 7

MINIATURE BULBS

The dainty dwarf species – Allium – Anemone – *Brodiaea grandiflora* – Chionodoxa – Crocus – Cyclamen – Eranthis – Erythronium – Galanthus – Iris – Leucojum – Muscari – Narcissus – *Puschkinia scilloides* – Scilla – *Triteleia uniflora* – Tulip – *Zephranthes candida* – Bulbs indoors.

THERE are no more valuable flowering plants for the tiny garden than the miniature bulbs, a number of which will provide bloom almost the whole year round. The larger flowering tulips and hyacinths are to be found in most gardens during spring and early summer but only very occasionally does one find the dainty species which will give almost as much colour from only a very limited space. Even more rarely are the delightful autumn and winter flowering species to be found and great is the loss, for bloom in the garden during the dull winter months will be more greatly appreciated than at any other time. There are so many dainty bulbs of such dwarf habit that several planted together, may occupy an area of no more than that enclosed by the circumference of a large cup and will provide several weeks of the most brilliant colouring. These charming bulbs may be planted in tiny beds, carpeted by the most dwarf of the primroses or double daises; about the rockery; in pots for the home and whose culture is described later; in a sink or window box; in small groups beneath trees or shrubs along a path, indeed almost anywhere, and the smaller the garden the more their beauty will be appreciated. Many of the miniature bulbs are indeed miniatures in every sense of the word, they are babies in comparison with the larger flowering varieties and yet are more than able to hold their own in the amount of colour they provide. They are also completely labour saving in that they may be left undisturbed for years.

Where it is required to use bulbs for inter-planting for small beds or window boxes and where they will be lifted after flowering, they may be grown in 3-in. pots, for then they may be planted and lifted without disturbing those plants which are grown with them. Planting should be exactly as where growing without pots, the rim of the pots being inserted just beneath soil level. After flowering the pots are placed on their sides as for bulbs grown indoors and in a cool, shaded place they will gradually die back. They should then be cleaned and stored in dry peat until ready for using again in autumn. Bulbs planted directly into open ground beds should be lifted with care after flowering and dried off in the same way, but wherever possible leave the bulbs undisturbed where many will multiply rapidly by means of offsets or from self-sown seed and quickly carpet the ground. This is the way in which the miniature bulbs are seen to best advantage. Surprisingly most of the true miniature bulbs remain unknown and yet most are so inexpensive.

ALLIUM. Though most of the flowering onions are suitable only for naturalizing or for the shrubbery or border, *A. Ostrowskianum* bears its deep rose-pink heads early in summer on only 5–6-in. stems. Planted in groups about a rockery or to the front of a small shrubbery the bulbs will provide colour when there is little other colour in the garden. Brought on in small pots, the bulbs may be used for a window box before the main summer display commences.

ANEMONE. Rarely are the Poppy anemones used for bedding, yet they provide a brilliance of colour over a long period rarely to be found with any other plant. Their fern-like foliage and cup-like blooms borne on 6–8-in. stems makes them an ideal plant for a small garden and if planted 6 in. apart they will quickly cover the ground with their bright green foliage. From an early autumn planting they will come into bloom early in summer and continue until the following autumn. They will then have a period of rest and if the ground has been well enriched with humus, will bloom again in spring. A hundred corms of the 2–3 cm. size, which is the best to use for bedding, the smaller corms being more vigorous, will cost about half a crown and will give masses of bloom for indoor or garden decoration. They are extremely hardy too, flourishing equally well in Cornish gardens and those of Northern Scotland, whilst the plants are extremely tolerant of the soot-laden atmosphere of a town. Plant the corms in early October, 1 in. deep, and because they are so small do not plant too close together. They quickly form masses of roots and make an abundance of foliage.

By using separate varieties, some delightful colour schemes may be enjoyed. Of the single or de Caen anemone, His Excellency bears a bloom of velvet-red with a striking white ring round the centre and is particularly attractive planted with The Bride, pure white with a black centre. Or plant with them, in circles or strips, the purple-blue Mr. Fokker. Of the double or St. Brigid anemones, The Governor bears a bloom of brilliant pillar-box red; Queen of Brilliance bears a cherry-red bloom; Lord Lieutenant, one of navy-blue; and Mount Everest, pure white.

The beautiful anemone species too remain sadly neglected, yet are an inexpensive method of providing masses of rich colour during spring and early summer. For massing as a carpet for daffodils, the exquisite rich blues of several of the species make them amongst the most beautiful flowers of the garden, and particularly do they thrive in a chalky soil. In a well-drained soil, planting may be done during late autumn, but where the soil is unduly heavy, this is better delayed until mid-March.

One of the first to bloom is *A. apennina*, which may quite easily be raised from seed or by root division immediately after flowering, though the most usual method is to plant tubers late in autumn. This is a charming plant for a shrub border or rockery, for the plants love the protection of stones. Its fern-like foliage appears as soon as the snow has gone, its single bright blue flowers with their golden centre appearing early in April and borne on 6-in. stems.

Equally hardy is *A. blanda*, the Grecian Windflower, which bears its deepest blue flowers on 4-in. stems during the first sunny days of spring. It is at its loveliest planted beneath silver birch trees, or on a bank of short grass beneath tall trees and where the sunshine may reach it. Possibly a miniature dell would suit it even better, for like all anemones it does not like cold winds. With the blue flowered *atrocoerulea*, plant the equally lovely *rosea*, which bears delicate rose-pink flowers.

A great lover of lime is the beautiful *A. ranunculoides*, which like the Winter Aconite bears its large cup-shaped blooms on 2-in. stems in March and has similar dark bronze foliage. This is a lovely plant for a rockery, where it should be planted in pockets of lime-rubble and where it will appreciate the protection of the stone. The best time to increase is by root division in autumn.

Equally lovely is the Silky Windflower or Pasque Flower, so named by the Elizabethan writer Gerard as it is always in bloom for Easter. It also enjoys similar conditions, a pocket about a rockery containing lime rubble and forming a long tap root it does not like disturbance. For this reason planting is best done from small pots in October where the soil is light, or in March where of a heavy nature. Propagation is by root cuttings, though the plants may readily be raised from seed in the same way as *A. alpina*, the last of the species to come into bloom. Being plants of the alpine regions, seed is sown during October in an outdoor bed enriched with leaf mould and some lime, and left entirely to the elements. These are the conditions the seed enjoys in its native Alpine regions. Germination takes place in spring and the seedlings should be potted in autumn or transplanted to flowering positions the following spring, at all times keeping the seedlings moist.

One of the loveliest varieties of *A. pulsatilla* is Letchworth Seedling, which bears a bloom of rich burgundy-red. Equally lovely is Budapest, found in Hungary, which bears a bloom of vivid lilac, whilst *rosea*, which received an Award of Merit in 1953, bears a bloom of strawberry-pink. The blooms are equally lovely in the bud stage, the outsides being covered with golden hairs.

A most handsome species in the Cyclamen-leaf Anemone which has large polished leaves and bears its handsome golden cup-shaped bloom during May. The plant prefers a position of full sun, but must have its roots in moisture, so appreciates a deep humus-laden soil. An equally fine plant is *A. vernalis*, called the Lady of the Snows, though in Britain it does not bloom until May. It has finely-cut foliage, its buds being violet-tinted and covered in golden hairs and opening to a silvery-white bloom of wax-like appearance.

All of them delightful plants for so many positions about the small garden and once established they should be left for years to give of their beauty.

BRODIAEA grandiflora. This charming bulb, bearing its bright blue flowers on 6-in. stems, blooms during early summer. It is hardy, but likes a sunny position and a well-drained soil containing grit. Plant in November, 2 in. apart and 1 in. deep for like all the miniature bulbs it resents too deep planting.

CHIONODOXA. All are very suitable for miniature gardening and are amongst the most brilliantly coloured flowers of spring. The bulbs may be planted about a rockery or shrubbery, in pots in window boxes, in the sink or trough garden, but preferably where they may be left undisturbed to reproduce themselves. Unlike the crocus they do not close up their blooms at the slightest breath of cold wind, whilst they remain quite untroubled by sleet showers.

C. sardensis is the first to come into bloom early in March, when it bears on 4–5-in. stems, its loose sprays of rich gentian-blue flowers with their vivid white centre. Then at the end of the month blooms *C. Luciliae*, of similar habit, with its brilliant blue flowers and glistening white centres. Not without good reason is it called the Glory of the Snow. There is also a pure white form, *C. Luciliae alba* and a rose-pink form, *C. Luciliae rosea*; whilst the new Pink Giant, flowering on 6-in. stems and bearing flowers of cyclamen-pink is enchanting. For April, *C. gigantea* bearing its large lavender-blue flowers on 5-in. stems, is very lovely. Planted with blue, purple or white winter-flowering pansies or with blue and white primroses, it is a delightful companion.

CROCUS. Whilst the autumn flowering colchicum with its coarse foliage is not suitable for miniature gardening, the many delightful species of the crocus, from those which come into bloom in September, the true autumn-flowering crocuses, to those which do not open their bloom until May, should be planted in as great a profusion as the size of garden will permit.

The first to bloom in early autumn is the showy *C. zonatus*, the bulbs costing only 2s. 6d. per dozen. It bears a thin, tapering bloom of rosy-lilac, coloured orange at the base. Then follows *C. speciosus*, its bright blue flowers having a brilliant orange stigma. There is a white form, *albus* whilst *Aitchisonii* bears a tapering bloom of a beautiful china-blue colour. In bloom at the same time is *C. pulchellus*, the lavender-blue flowers having white anthers. For early October, *C. medius* bearing deep purple blooms and *C. longiflorus*, delicate mauve are followed by *C. ochroleucus* and *C. niveus*, their glistening white blooms looking particularly bright during the dull days of November.

C. Imperati will bear its scented fawn and violet blooms for Christmas. Then, whenever there is a mild day towards the end of January, *C. Fleischeri* comes into bloom. Its striking small white flower with its orange-scarlet stigma is delightful in a window box planted with the wine coloured winter pansies. In February *C. Korolkowi*, with its vivid golden flowers comes into bloom. Then in March comes the handsome *C. Corsicus*, with its large bold flowers of deep cream and purple; and *C. susianus*, glossy gold and brown. At the same time the lovely *C. chrysanthus* varieties are also in bloom. E. A. Bowles, with its handsome canary-yellow flowers is lovely; also the creamy-white Snow Bunting. In April *C. Thomasianus* opens its lovely sapphire-blue flowers. The new variety, Taplow Ruby, wine-purple, is quite outstanding. Even later to bloom is *C. Olivieri*, with its tubular blooms of brilliant orange-yellow, the last crocus to flower.

Of the Dutch or large-flowered hybrids, Vanguard comes early into bloom with its flowers of grey and mauve. Equally lovely is Queen of the Blues, silvery-purple; whilst Paulus Potter bears a huge bloom of ruby-purple. Plant as a companion, either the pure white Snowstorm, or Barr's Golden-Yellow.

Where possible plant a few bulbs of a number of the species close together so that there will be a succession of bloom. They are most attractive planted in grass which is cut for the last time at the end of August or where this is not practical, then cut about October 1st, and plant those which come first into bloom in November. Utilizing a small lawn in this way will be a means of providing additional colour where space is strictly limited.

CYCLAMEN. The hardy autumn and spring flowering cyclamen are excellent plants for a tiny garden, planted around the roots of an old tree, on a rockery or at the foot of an old wall for they love shelter from midday sun and cold winds. The beautiful glossy foliage attractively veined or marbled adds to their beauty and provides a valuable ground cover for other bulbs. They like some lime rubble mixed into the soil before planting, the corms being set only 1 in. deep and 6–8 in. apart.

Of neat, compact habit is *C. cilicicium*, its dark green leaves having a silvery zone, whilst its flowers are pale pink. Also flowering early in autumn is *C. europeum*, its foliage being mottled with silver, its crimson flowers being sweetly scented. Coming into bloom several weeks later is *C. neapolitanum*, which has silver marbled foliage and bears deep pink flowers which are produced before its foliage.

For early spring flowering, *C. coum* with its round dark green leaves and crimson flowers and its white flowered counterpart, *album*, is a charming plant, and for May, plant *C. repandum*, which has silvery foliage and bears bright crimson-red flowers.

ERANTHIS. Planted along a path, around the base of dwarf trees, about a shrubbery, indeed almost anywhere, the Winter Aconite provides a most welcome splash of colour during February and March, their beautiful golden cups nestling amidst attractive fern-like foliage. *E. hyemalis* bears its golden cups amidst bright green foliage, whilst *E. cilicica* bears a larger and more deeply-coloured bloom amidst bronze foliage and is a little later to bloom. Plant the bulbs where they will not be disturbed, spacing them 4 in. apart and planting 1½ in. deep.

ERYTHRONIUM. There are no more beautiful plants for early spring flowering than the Dog's Tooth Violets, so called because of their violet-like blooms and because their bulbs are the shape of a canine tooth. Like the eranthis and hardy cyclamen, they may be planted anywhere about the garden, but they like a soil enriched with some peat or leaf mould. They should be planted 3 in. deep in October, spacing them about 6 in. apart. Mixed bulbs of *E. dens-canis* will produce blooms of rose, pink, purple and white which hover like butterflies on 4-in. stems above glossy deep green foliage, veined with silver. Neither cold winds nor snow will harm them and the bulbs cost only 7s. 6d. per dozen. Rather more expensive but one of the most beautiful plants of the garden is *E. tuolumnensis*, which has dark green foliage above which it bears its golden-yellow blooms on 9-in. stems.

GALANTHUS. Better known as the Snowdrop and everybody's favourite. On a low grassy bank, about a lawn or shrub border, indeed planted anywhere, no bloom is more welcome and with the melting of the snow their beauty is revealed. They should be planted where they are to be left undisturbed to reproduce themselves from seed, or they may be lifted immediately after flowering and divided and replanted. Each of the species are lovely and outstanding is *G. Imperati Atkinsi*, which will bear its large, snow-white tubes on

8-in. stems soon after Christmas. At its best during February is *G. nivalis*, which is the familiar green-tipped snowdrop. The double form *flore pena* is rather later to bloom. For March flowering is *G. Elwesii*, with its attractive grey foliage and large flowers with their vivid green inner segments held on 6–7-in. stems, is an excellent variety.

IRIS. For window box or trough, for the rockery or for planting in grass or along a path there is no plant so hardy and so easy to grow as the delightful little *I. reticulata*, and several other dwarf species. They come into bloom with the first warm rays of the spring sunshine, towards the end of February or early March and making almost no foliage and with their upright habit require only the minimum of room in which to display their charms. Like the hardy cyclamen, the dwarf irises like a soil containing lime rubble but enjoy a more open situation. Plant in October 2 in. deep and to produce a rich display, plant in circular groups of six bulbs, spacing them 2–3 in. apart.

The first to bloom and most charming is *I. Danfordiae*, which bears its bright golden blooms before the end of February. Then comes *I. histrioides major*, the quite large blooms are borne on 6–8-in. stems. The purple-blue flowers have a conspicuous white blotch on the fall petals.

During March and early April *I. reticulata* is in bloom, its sweetly fragrant flowers borne on 8–9-in. stems. The blooms are deep violet-purple with a striking yellow blotch on the fall. Possibly lovelier is the new Cantab, which has pale blue standards and rather deeper coloured fall petals which are attractively marked with a golden crest. As a companion, Royal Blue, which may be described as a pure Oxford-blue colour, the fall petals having the same conspicuous golden blotch, is equally lovely.

LEUCOJUM. It is the Spring Snowflake, *L. vernum*, which grows to a height of 6 in. that is suitable for the miniature garden. Several pretty drooping bells which are white, attractively tipped with green are borne on each stem during April. They are at their best when massed on the rockery or in grass. They like a soil containing some humus, when they will multiply rapidly if left undisturbed.

MUSCARI. This is the Grape Hyacinth so called because of its dainty hyacinth-like spikes of tiny grape-like flowers. For naturalizing with the dwarf daffodils and wild primroses with the yellow blooms they make a charming contrast. If left undisturbed, the muscari will rapidly increase and form dense purple-blue carpets from March until the end of May. The first to bloom is *M. azurem*, its spikes of bright Cambridge-blue being borne on 6-in. stems. Plant together the equally lovely pure white form, *album*. The well-known free-flowering hybrid Heavenly Blue, slightly taller growing and bearing its fragrant gentian-blue flowers throughout April, is equally attractive and this is followed by the new hybrid, Cantab, of similar habit and bearing attractive pale blue flowers. The latest to bloom is *M. polyanthum album* which bears handsome spikes of pure white bells on 6-in. stems, remaining more than a month in bloom.

NARCISSUS. For the small garden for planting beneath young trees and shrubs, for a rockery, small window box or trough garden, the miniature daffodils are enchanting. They may require a season to become fully established for they hate disturbance, but will then literally carpet the ground with their fairy-like bloom which dances in the late spring breezes for weeks on end. They are at their best planted about a grassy bank or lawn though no grass cutting should be done until their foliage has died down at the end of June. If planted about a shrubbery or rockery 3–4 in. deep, it will be possible to clean the ground above them in midsummer after the foliage has died back. They are seen to best advantage if planted with the grape hyacinths which will bloom and die back at the same time. Both plants like an ordinary soil but it must be well drained in winter.

The earliest and most dwarf of all daffodils is surely *N. minimus*, which bears its tiny yellow trumpets on only 3-in. stems and comes into bloom before the end of February. Almost as early is *N. minor*, which bears its yellow-lobed trumpet on 5-in. stems early in March. At the same time blooms *N. cyclamineus*, the Cyclamen flowered Daffodil, so called because its golden trumpet is reflexed like a cyclamen bloom. It grows to a height of 6 in. A lovely hybrid is February Gold which has a lemon-yellow perianth and a frilled orange trumpet. It is rather taller growing, but another hybrid Beryl, which has a pale yellow perianth and orange cup, blooms on only 8-in. stems.

One of the loveliest of the miniatures is *N. canaliculatus*, a tiny polyanthus narcissus which bears four sweetly-scented flowers to each 6-in. stem above erect blue-green foliage towards the end of March. At the same time the Hoop Petticoat daffodil, *N. bulbocodium conspicuous*, is in bloom, its little rounded flowers of golden-yellow born on 6-in. stems above rush-like foliage. The Angel's Tears daffodil, *N. triandus albus*, bears a cluster of drooping globular creamy white blooms at the same time and at a similar height. Towards the end of April *N. tenuiar* is in bloom. It is known as the Silver Jonquil and bears two or three deliciously fragrant blooms of cream and pale yellow on 8-in. stems. Last to bloom is *N. gracilis*, one of the loveliest of all though it grows to a height of 12 in. It bears as many as five pale yellow Jonquil-like blooms to each stem during the last days of May and is richly fragrant.

PUSCHKINIA scilloides. The Lebanon Squill is a delightful little April flowering plant which grows to a height of only 6 in. The blooms are white, striped pale blue, several of which are borne at the end of each stem. It requires much the same culture as the scillas, a position where the bulbs will receive some sunshine to ripen, without which they will not bloom well. William Robinson, the Victorian authority on flowers, described this as "one of the prettiest plants of the garden".

SCILLA. It is the spring flowering Squill which bears its tiny spikes at a height of only 4 in. which is suitable for a trough, rockery or shrubbery. It likes a more sunny position than the English and Spanish scillas, the Bluebells. The first to bloom is *S. bifolia*, in the blue and shell-pink forms, followed by *S. sibirica*, towards the end of April. The Siberian Squill bears short spikes of blue or white flowers. Nor should the Dalmatian species be neglected. This is *S. amethystina*, which produces spikes of deep purple-blue flowers towards the end of May on 6-in. stems. The squills should be planted 3 in. deep and in a soil containing some humus.

TRITELIA uniflora. This is the Spring Star Flower, a most charming plant which, during April, bears lavender star-like flowers which have a violet stripe down each petal. The bulbs should be planted 3 in. deep to protect them from frost and it prefers a permanent position. The blooms are borne on 6-in. stems.

TULIP. Whilst it may not be possible to find a place in the miniature garden for the taller flowering Darwin and Cottage tulips, the Single and Double tulips and a number of the interesting species will be most suitable and will provide rich colour from the appearance in March of *T. turkestanica*, until May when *T. linifolius* comes into bloom. For window boxes and for planting 4 in. apart in small beds where they give a brilliant display during April and May, the single and double early flowering tulips are of the easiest culture. They should be planted in early November, the last of all the spring flowering bulbs and they will be happy in any ordinary soil. They are at their best in slightly raised beds, using two contrasting colours and selecting only those varieties of dwarf habit, which bloom on 11–12-in. stems. In the single varieties Sunburst, brilliant yellow flushed orange; Olympiade, pure golden-yellow; and the lovely white, Diana are excellent for small beds, whilst in the doubles, Van der Hoef, pure yellow; Dante, blood-red; and Peach Blossom, peach-pink are also of compact habit.

Many of the species, almost unknown amongst tulip lovers are of more dainty habit and suitable for troughs and for a rockery, also for planting in short grass. The species are generally longer lived than the large flowered varieties and if left undisturbed will rapidly increase. The earliest to bloom and of dainty habit is *T. turkestanica*, which bears cream coloured flowers, flushed with bronze and green, on short branched stems. In a sunny position it is in bloom from early March. In bloom shortly after is *T. pulchella*, a beauty amongst miniature flowers. It bears, on 5-in. stems, charming urn-shaped flowers of deepest purple. Early in April blooms *T. Clusiana* on 8-in. stems. The outer petals are cherry-red, the inner petals being white. The bulbs should be planted 6 in. deep, close to crazy paving or rockery stone. In bloom at the same time is another gem for the rock garden, *T. dasystemon*, which bears numerous canary-yellow blooms to each 6-in. stem. Towards the end of April *T. chrysantha* comes into bloom, its deep yellow flowers being shaded cherry-red on the outside. One of the most colourful of the species is *T. praestans*, being rather taller growing and which bears three or four brilliant orange flowers to each stem.

There are a number of May flowering species which will prolong the season into the first weeks of summer. Flowering on only 6-in. stems the dainty *T. linifolia* bears glowing scarlet blooms which have a purple centre; whilst *T. persica*, the smallest of all tulips, bears its brilliant yellow fragrant blooms on only 3-in. stems.

For a window box, rockery or for planting in small beds, the brilliantly coloured early flowering Kaufmanniana tulips are outstandingly beautiful. Natives of Central Asia, they open their huge polished blooms before the end of March and remain long in bloom. The species bears a creamy-white bloom with broad petals which are shaded with red on the outside. It grows to a height of only 6 in. and bears as large a bloom as do the Darwin and Cottage tulips. An even dwarfer form of exquisite beauty is the variety Gaiety, the deep cream coloured blooms, striped red on the outside, almost resting on the ground. Outstanding too, is *T. Kaufmanniana aurea*, the blooms being like cups of golden yellow with the outside of the petals deepest scarlet. Beautiful and of dwarf habit is the variety Shakespeare, the blooms being of a blend of apricot and salmon, whilst *coccinea* bears a bloom of deepest crimson. Just two or three planted together will provide richer colouring than any other plant in the garden and at a time when there are few other brightly coloured flowers.

ZEPHRANTHES candida. A most valuable and beautiful plant, producing in autumn a profusion of pure white, crocus-like flowers on 8-in. stems. It requires a sunny position, though a soil which is retentive of summer moisture. It is a delightful plant for a rockery or for planting along a path or as an edging to a shrubbery.

Bulbs Indoors

Almost all the miniature bulbs described in this chapter may be grown indoors, though it is those which bloom during the winter and early spring which will be more greatly appreciated. Contrary to expectations, it may generally be said of the dwarf flowering bulbs that they should be given a longer time to form their roots than the large flowered tulips, daffodils and hyacinths. In other words, they resent forcing in any way and especially before they have become well rooted. Those to bloom, like the crocuses, in the early winter months should be potted in July. They should be placed in a cool, shaded corner away from the sun's rays and should be covered to a depth of at least 6 in. with ashes or sand. This will be found to be a more satisfactory method of encouraging a strong root formation than to place the pots in a cupboard or the drawer of a room where conditions are almost always too dry and warm, the bulbs being started into partial growth before being thoroughly rooted. Bulbs to bloom in the early New Year and spring should be potted in early September and if possible should be placed in the open and covered as deeply as possible with ashes or sand. A sand and peat mixture is also excellent. The bulbs obtain sufficient natural moisture to keep them comfortably moist, yet they should not be placed where water constantly drips on to them. They should be left undisturbed until the end of November, when the covering should be removed with care and the pots or bowls taken indoors. Here, they should be placed in a cool, semi-shaded position for a fortnight to become slowly acclimatized to their new surroundings, but at no time should they be given excessive warmth. They should be grown on in a cool, buoyant atmosphere, the compost being kept comfortably moist but in no way saturated.

Where the bulbs are to be given their rooting period indoors, a cellar is ideal for them though generally the place chosen will be under the stairs or in a cupboard, which will provide the requisite darkness, though the warmth will often cause the compost to dry out too rapidly. The result is that bulbs suffer where attention is not given to the moisture requirements or one goes to the other extreme and provides more than the bulbs, with their limited root action, can use, and so causing the roots to decay. If the compost is kept too dry plant growth will be stunted and the blooms will be inconspicuous and often deformed. The moisture of the compost should be neither excessive nor too little, whilst the bulbs should be kept as cool as possible whilst rooting. The more vigorous the root action, the better will be the display of bloom.

The compost for indoor bulbs also frequently causes trouble, for unless made thoroughly moist before it is used, bulb fibre is rarely able to take in sufficient moisture afterwards. The bulbs, therefore, never make sufficient root growth. The pots must be crocked to ensure satisfactory drainage, and this is even more important where a bowl is being used and which will generally be without a drainage hole. Bulb fibre may be used if made thoroughly moist, but more satisfactory will be to use moist peat to which has been incorporated some clean turf loam and a small quantity of grit. The loam will help to retain moisture and give "body" to the compost.

Small pots which will hold three bulbs may be used and will be most attractive, likewise earthenware seed pans, which will accommodate half a dozen small bulbs. No great depth of soil is required provided there is sufficient for the bulbs to make substantial root growth and prevent too rapid moisture evaporation. The bulbs should be planted no more than 1 in. below soil level.

Chapter 8

MINIATURE TREES AND SHRUBS

Preparing the ground for shrubs – Deciduous shrubs for a small border – Evergreen shrubs – Dwarf conifers.

AMONGST the most useful plants for a small garden are the miniature trees and shrubs, for besides their value on the rockery and for troughs, where planted in small groups they form a delightful background for small flowering plants. Most attractive are those dwarf shrubs which grow less than 3 ft. tall and which may be used to form a small shrub border about which the miniature bulbs may be planted. These dwarf shrubs are charming when used for raised beds bordered by a stone wall about 2 ft. high. In this way the plants will be revealed to their best advantage and will form a permanent part of the tiny garden. Even where there is no garden, it is possible to make a shrubbery by tipping quantities of drainage materials and loam over a stone or asphalt base to be found in most small yards and which will otherwise grow little. In place of small trees and shrubs, the bed, which should be raised about 2 ft. above ground level, may be planted with miniature roses, with summer flowering annuals or with dwarf begonias and geraniums, the dwarf conifers being used as a background.

A low wall may quite easily be made by a handyman using pre-cast concrete "stones", or cut stone which will be considerably more expensive. Second hand bricks may also be used, the older the better so as to provide a more pleasing appearance. The side or corner of the yard should be selected which will receive as much sunshine as possible and full advantage should be taken of the sun's rays by washing the walls of the yard with Snowcem. The low wall should be built in proportion to the size of the yard and to a design determined by the shape of the yard. Where there is an entrance, this too must be taken into consideration. Most yards have storage sheds for coal, dustbins, and other necessary conveniences, and these will also dictate the shape and position of the raised bed.

Making Up the Bed

Though a wall which is slightly curved will be more pleasing to the eye, it will also be more difficult to build and the novice should use straight lines. Where a garden is of sufficient size to permit a more pretentious use to be made of stone and raised beds, professional labour might be employed. The stone arch illustrated in this book was erected in a garden of small dimensions and which was of almost triangular shape. The apex of the triangle was isolated by the neat archway flanked by low raised beds. From the arch was made a small path of crazy paving stone leading to a gate, the raised beds being planted with dwarf shrubs and trees, including evergreens which remained colourful all the year round. The remainder of the garden was occupied by a small lawn, the entire area being surrounded by inter-woven wooden fencing. The

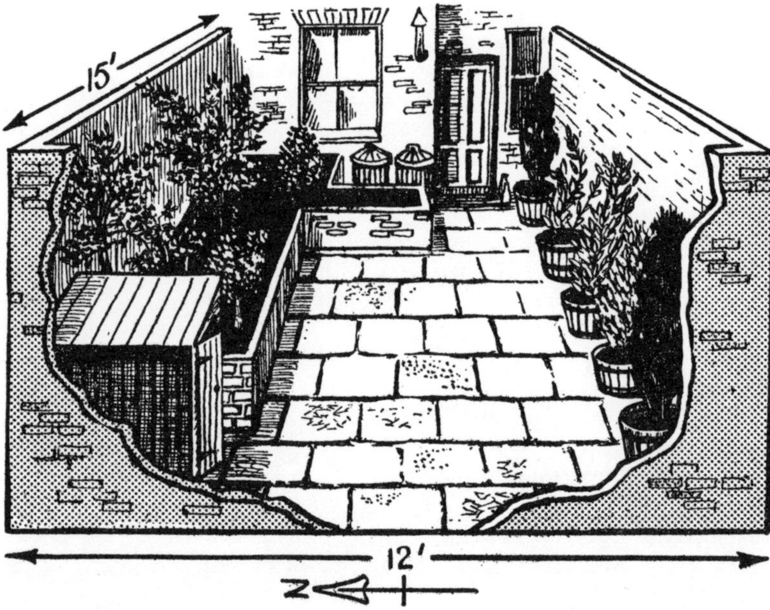

whole had a simple attractiveness and was entirely labour saving and permanent, only the cutting of the grass requiring attention. The "stone" archway and wrought iron gate give a "continental" appearance whilst bringing to the small garden a feeling of greater space. Where there is no natural background of trees, silver birches, neat and colourful throughout the year with their silver bark, should be planted close to the fence, or possibly those conifers of most upright habit could be used.

It is important to give the wall a solid foundation, concrete first being laid to a depth of 2–3 in. Apart from building the wall level and straight, which is done by using lines and a spirit level, the work calls for no great experience unless an intricate design is required. When the wall has been erected, it will be necessary to provide soil and drainage materials to the depth of the wall. To a depth of about 6 in., crushed brick or stone should be placed over which cinders are scattered. Then, to a depth of 12 in. add soil of a heavy loamy nature and in which stones have not been removed. Stones will also help to provide efficient drainage whilst the soil should be pressed well down so that no air pockets remain. The top 6 in. should consist of screened loam to which has been incorporated some decayed manure or peat and 2 oz. of bone meal per square yard. The bed should be allowed a fortnight to settle before any planting is done.

Where a miniature shrubbery is to be made on the flat, a clay soil should be broken up by first dressing with caustic lime. After two weeks, pulverised brick, grit or very coarse sand should be worked into the soil together with some decayed manure, peat or used hops when after several more days have passed, planting may take place.

Where the soil is light and sandy, considerable quantities of humus should be incorporated, though drainage materials will not be necessary.

Whilst the deciduous trees and shrubs may be moved at any time between early November and early March, the conifers and evergreens should only be moved in early springtime, during the month of March when just starting into growth. No planting, however, should be done whilst the soil is wet and sticky or when it is frosted. Again, whilst deciduous trees may be moved with little or no soil about their roots, the conifers should retain as much soil as possible for they resent disturbance at any time. If obtaining conifers from a distance, they should be sent with their roots wrapped in sacking to prevent drainage and too great a loss of soil. If received whilst the ground is unfit for planting, stand them in a cool shed, whilst the deciduous trees should be placed in a trench until ready to plant. Always plant firmly, treading round the roots and water well if the soil appears dry.

Deciduous shrubs for a Small Border

AMYGDALUS nana. Sometimes known as the dwarf almond, it makes a dwarf shrub increased in size by underground stems. It bears a mass of bright rose-coloured flowers in spring.

BEECH. All are slow growing but *Fagus asplenifolia* takes many years to attain a height of 5 ft. Its foliage is most graceful, being cut into narrow fronds. Ideal as a specimen tree in a tiny garden or for the back of a shrub border.

BERBERIS. Almost all are evergreen, but two are deciduous

and of dwarf compact habit. *B. Sieboldii*, of tufted form has glossy leaves marbled with crimson and which take on brilliant crimson tints in autumn, whilst *B. Wilsonae* of similar habit, bears beautiful coral-pink berries in autumn.

CHERRY. A number of the ornamental cherries, members of the large *prunus* family are of dwarf habit and most suitable for a tiny garden. Not only is their blossom most attractive in early summer, but their foliage takes on the richest colours of autumn whilst their bark remains colourful throughout the year. *Prunus litigiosa* rarely exceeds a height of 3–4 ft., forming a dense pyramid and bearing pendant white blossoms.

P. Subhirtella rubra pendula, a lovely wild species, grows to a similar height, its weeping branches being covered with ruby-red blooms during April. In bloom at the same time is *P. Sieboldii*, of upright habit and producing its double shell-pink flowers in early spring. Extremely valuable in that it blooms during the depth of winter is *P. Fudan-Sakura*, from Japan. It makes a low, broad shrub, its blooms being shining white.

CLEMATIS. Quite distinct from the well-known climbing forms is Côte d'Azur, which forms a spreading bush only 2–3 ft. high. In autumn it bears its candelabras of tiny delicate blue flowers which are especially appreciated when, apart from foliage, there is little colour in the shrubbery at this time.

COTONEASTER. C. horizontalis variegata is a most dainty plant to cover a low wall. It grows only 2 ft. tall and is of fan-shape, its tiny leaves being silvery-green. The arching *C. decora* is just as dainty and bears large white flowers followed by scarlet berries.

CYDONIA japonica. With its clusters of brilliantly coloured flowers in spring which appear before the foliage and which are followed by fruits which make delicious jelly, the flowering quinces make ideal plants for a small shrubbery or for covering a low wall. All are slow growing, two being particularly so. *C. rosea plena* bears large double pink flowers and grows to a height of only 2½ ft., whilst *C. Maulei*, from China is even more dwarf and bears bright salmon coloured flowers followed by golden fruit.

CYTISUS. The dwarf "brooms" are excellent plants for a dry, sandy soil and a position of full sun. *C. Kewensis* makes a low arching bush and bears cream coloured flowers, whilst *C. Ardoinei* is a miniature which grows only 6–8 in. high and bears exquisite golden flowers.

DAPHNE. These superb early spring flowering plants like a cool, moist soil, one containing some humus and as cool a position as possible though sheltered from early spring winds. *D. Blagayana*, which prefers some shade, is of almost trailing habit and bears its fragrant cream coloured flowers in April. *D. Collina* makes but a tiny bush and bears its rosy-red flowers in June. Of more dwarf habit than *D. Mezereum* is *D. Onearum* which forms a compact cushion completely hidden by the fragrant pink flowers during May. It likes plenty of humus in the soil and takes some little time to become established.

FORSYTHIA. Indispensable for their sprays of golden bells in early spring and which appear before the foliage, *F. Bronxensis* makes only a low, spreading bush 12 in. high compared with a height of 6 ft. attained by the other species and varieties.

HEDYSARUM multijugum. An unusual and almost unknown dwarf shrub which grows to a height of less than 3 ft. Throughout July it bears its tapering spires of purple vetch-like flowers and has vivid green foliage.

LIQUIDAMBAR. It rarely exceeds a height of 6 ft. and is ideal for the back of a small shrub border. Its maple-like foliage takes on the most brilliant crimson and orange tints in autumn, the foliage being retained until almost the year end.

MAPLE. Several of the maples with their beautiful foliage and extreme tolerance of town conditions may be recommended, and none is lovelier than *Acer dissectum* of dwarf, spreading habit, its finely-laced foliage being of a bright green colour. Also growing only 2 ft. tall and of similar habit is *A. dissectum purpureum*, which has chestnut coloured foliage which turns vivid scarlet in autumn. Plant the two together. They are most suitable for the roof garden of a town house where grown in tubs.

MOUNTAIN ASH. The charming little *Sorbus reducta*, which grows only 2 ft. tall and bears masses of scarlet berries is ideal for a tiny shrubbery.

PHILADELPHUS. There is a lovely "mock orange" which grows no taller than 12 in. and is a superb plant for a rockery. Its name is Manteau d'Hermine and it covers its slender branches with deliciously fragrant white flowers during July.

POTENTILLA. The shrubby potentillas are extremely attractive. They form dwarf, tiny bushes 12–10 in. high, on which they bear their clusters of strawberry-like flowers on short branched stems. *P. Beesii* growing only 10–12 in. tall, has attractive silver foliage and bears golden-yellow flowers whilst *P. mandschurica*, also having silvery foliage bears pure white flowers over a long period.

RIBES alpinum. This is the miniature form of the flowering currant, bearing pale green flowers, but it is for its rich golden foliage that it should be grown. It will grow no taller than 10 in. and remain compact without attention.

SYRINGA microphylla. This is a tiny Japanese lilac rarely reaching more than 18 in. in height and which bears its purple sprays of bloom in early summer.

WEIGELA. June flowering and quite happy in poor soils, *W. rosea variegata* makes a rounded bush 2 ft. in height, has bright silver striped foliage and bears pretty pink flowers, whilst *W. foliis purpureis* has attractive purple leaves and bears rose-pink flowers.

Evergreen Shrubs

AZALEA Kurume. With their shiny box-like foliage and tiny but richly coloured flowers this is the most dwarf of the azalea family, attaining a height of about 15 in. Like all the family, they require a peaty lime-free soil. The Kurume azaleas bloom throughout April and amongst the best are Esmeralda, soft pink and double; Hatsugiri, heather-purple; and Orange Beauty.

BERBERIS. The many berberis species are excellent plants for a shady garden and are extremely varied in form. Some, though dwarf, have a loose habit whilst others are very compact and amongst these is *B. buxifolia nana*, which has glossy box-like foliage and bears large golden flowers. Of similar habit, *B. chrysosphaera* also has glossy leaves and bears lemon-yellow flowers.

Though *B. stenophylla* is vigorous growing, most of the forms are extremely compact. Crawley Beauty makes a compact little hummock and bears salmon coloured flowers, whilst *coccinea*, with its scarlet flowers has a fountain-like form as of a firework in display.

Cistus. The evergreen rock roses, in bloom from mid-June until mid-August thrive in poor, sandy soils and in a position of full sun whilst no plant blooms more freely. All are of dwarf habit though several more so than others. Of these, *C. carbariensis* is one of the hardiest. It grows to a height of 20 in., its pure white blooms appearing most attractively against its dark green foliage. Excellent too, is *C. Ingwersenianus* also white flowering and of almost prostrate habit.

ERICA. A number of the lime-tolerant heaths and those of compact habit are excellent plants for the front of a border. They bloom from November until the end of April, each flowering for about two months. The first to bloom are members of the *E. carnea* group, especially the crimson flowered Ruby Gem and *praecox rubra*. Then follows the white flowered C. M. Beale and later come Vivelli, red and the Springwoods, Pink and White. All attain a height of less than 12 in. During February and March *E. darleyensis* bears its long spikes of warm pink on 15-in. stems and at the same time *E. hibernica coccinea*, rose-crimson is in bloom. For mid-winter colour too, Silver Mist bearing its spikes of silver-white at Christmas and the almost black-leaved William Rackliffe, also white flowered are two beautiful plants.

ESCALLONIA. Delightful plants with their shiny dark green foliage and are especially happy in coastal districts. They bear their clusters of blossom for weeks on end and a number form low, bushy plants 2½ ft. tall. They have an additional value in that they are fully evergreen. William Watson is extremely dwarf and bears crimson-red flowers, whilst Peach Blossom bears bloom of a lovely shade of peach-pink.

RHODODENDRON. A number of the dwarf hybrids are charming plants. They like a lime-free soil and should be planted about a shrubbery or rockery in pockets of peat. They are expensive, costing at least half a guinea each but are extremely beautiful and long lasting. The most dwarf is one of the loveliest, *R. Lanceanum nanum*, which bears its tubular flowers of lemon-yellow during April at a height of only 6–8 in. Only slightly taller growing is *R. racemosum*, which bears clusters of shell-pink flowers in spring, whilst *R. impeditum* bears its amethyst-blue bells at the same time. To prolong the season, plant *R. keleticum*, which bears crimson-purple flowers in June, likewise *R. brachyanthum*, which bears lemon-yellow flowers.

ROSEMARY. The most compact forms of this lovely old-world plant are Miss Jessop's Upright and Severn Seas, which bear their smoky-blue flowers in spring. Both forms are neat and of upright habit and grow no more than 2 ft. tall. The rosemary likes a dry, sandy soil and a sunny position.

SENECIO GRAYI compacta. It makes a neat, rounded bush with wavy, dark grey leaves and bears yellow daisy-like flowers from mid-June until October. It is extremely hardy and tolerant of salt winds.

VERONICA. With their glossy leaves, long flowering period and compact habit, the shrubby veronicas are most suited to the small garden and especially one situated near the coast. Excellent is the new Bowle's Variety, which makes a compact shrub 20 in. tall and bears its pale lilac blooms, like fluffy spikes, from early summer until winter. Similar in every way is Warley Pink. More dwarf is *V. Pageana*, which has grey foliage and white flower spikes, whilst *V. Hectori* has bright golden foliage and though it doesn't bloom it provides a pleasing contrast in the shrubbery.

Dwarf Conifers

Those growing to between 1½–2½ ft. tall and which are suitable for a tiny garden, for planting in small groups, will be described here, those of even more dwarf habit and suitable for a rockery or trough garden are described in Chapter 12.

ABIES lasiocarpa compacta. It will eventually reach a height of 2 ft. and is of conical habit, the foliage being silver-grey with attractive brown buds.

CEDRUS Deodara. It is of almost weeping form, making a dense, low, bushy tree of feathery pale green foliage, the shoots recurving at the tips.

CEDRUS Sargenti pendula. Of more dwarf habit that *C. deodara,* it makes a low, rounded bush of weeping form.

CUPRESSUS Lawsoniana. With their dense, shaggy foliage, members of this family are slow growing and most compact. *Cupressus nana glauca* grows to a height of 2 ft. forming a densely-branched dark green tree. Plant with it *C. nana aurea,* of similar habit but having bright golden foliage. The variety, *Ellwoodii,* which will eventually attain a height of 5 ft. makes a dense little pyramid, pointed at the top, the foliage being of a rich grey-green.

CUPRESSUS obtusa. Members of the family have dense growth and a conical habit, and one of the best is *C. gracilis,* which will attain a height of 2 ft. and has curving branches of bright green feathery foliage. *C. tetragona aurea* has almost moss-like foliage of vivid gold and is happiest in partial shade; whilst *C. spiralis* has attractively cupped-shaped branches.

JUNIPERUS. The Junipers have a more diverse habit than any of the conifers, some being of columnar form whilst others spread out their branches almost horizontally. Those which are of almost pencil-like habit should be planted in groups of two or three. One of the best is Irish Juniper, *J. communis hibernica,* which forms a pencil-like column of blue-grey. Of similar habit is the Chinese Juniper, *J. chinensis* whose foliage turns a lovely mulberry shade during winter.

Of the more horizontal forms, *J. sabina tamariscifolia,* the Carpet Juniper, is of spreading habit and has attractive tamarisk-like foliage. With its pretty arching branches, and blue-grey foliage which turns silver-grey in winter, *J. squamata Meyeri* is an outstanding species.

PICEA excelsa. These are the dwarf spruces, which are low growing and have thick horizontal branches with blue-green foliage. One of the best is *P. Ramontii,* of pyramidal habit, the lower branches sitting on the ground whilst the foliage is of a rich bottle-green colour. Also excellent is *P. nana compacta,* the dwarf form of the Norway Spruce, the horizontally spreading branches giving it a globular appearance. No conifer has more richly coloured foliage than *P. glauco-procumbens,* being bright silvery-blue, whilst *P. Veitchi* forms a dwarf rounded tree with bright olive-green foliage.

PINUS. The dwarf pines, with their thick trunks and clusters of leaves are quite charming. *P. Watereriana,* like a miniature Scots Pine with its bright brown trunk and blue-grey needles is most charming; whilst *P. argenta pumila* has long needles of pale grey.

TAXUS. The dwarf yews are extremely slow growing and most

charming and none more so than the golden weeping form of the English Yew, *T. baccata Dovastonii aurea*. *T. cuspidata nana* is even more dwarf and spreading so that when the tree has attained a height of 2 ft., its branches will cover an area more than 12 in. in diameter. *T. Standishi* is a beautiful little yew of upright habit, its foliage being bright golden-yellow.

THUYA. Delightful evergreens growing broader than they grow tall and having dainty, feathery foliage. *T. occidentalis* has green foliage which turns bronzy-red in winter, whilst *T. aurea globosa* is even more globular in form, its golden foliage becoming rich bronze in autumn. *T. laetivirens* is a charming little tree, happy in shade, its foliage being like moss.

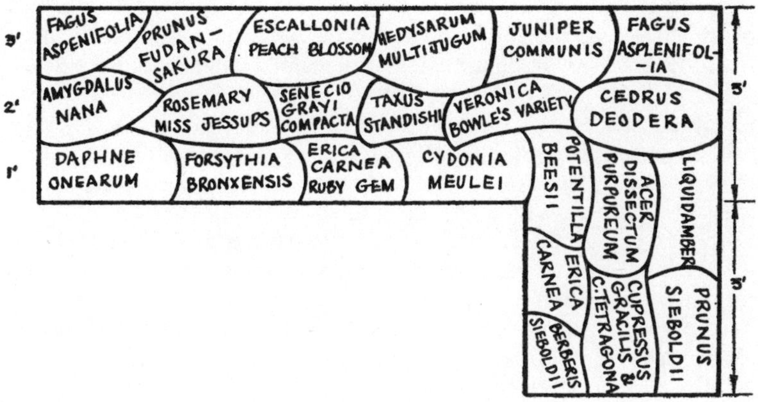

A Border of Dwarf Shrubs

Chapter 9

DWARF HEDGES

The value of low hedges – Care of a dwarf hedge – Suitable plants for a miniature hedge.

A SMALL garden may be made additionally attractive by the use of small hedges, some being of miniature proportions. They may be planted to surround small beds which are to be filled with spring and summer bedding plants, or they may be used on either side of a path, or to edge a border of shrubs or herbaceous plants. The dwarf hedging plants provide a neater appearance where used in this way than do most hardy plants so often used in a similar way. If kept nicely trimmed, they will retain their dwarf habit whilst they will not fall over the edges of path or lawn, causing the stone to become mossy or the grass to die back. And with their sturdy, erect habit they will not occupy anything like as much ground as will most flowering plants used for edging. A dwarf hedge will also provide shelter from cold winds and where the garden is in any way exposed, serious thought should be given to the planting of a miniature hedge. Well cared for, dwarf hedges add charm and interest to any garden. They were widely used in Tudor days, small beds of violets and primroses and other sweet smelling flowers being surrounded with dwarf hedges of box or lavender, the beds being made into pleasing designs with the smallest garden taking on a new charm. Once planted, the dwarf hedge will be permanent and will keep the garden neat and tidy and being evergreen, they will provide a colour during those flowerless periods. Small beds of the miniature roses look most charming when enclosed by a dwarf hedge, so do violas and primroses, the multiflora begonias and dwarf geraniums.

Care of a Hedge

Whilst the plants selected for a dwarf hedge should be slow growing it is possible to keep those which are more vigorous, compact and tidy by careful and constant clipping. The more clipping the plants receive the more bushy will they become close to the ground, which is the hall-mark of a low hedge. A hedge of any description which is bare at the base will prove inefficient and have an untidy appearance. It will, therefore, be necessary to clip it from the beginning to encourage bushy growth at ground level. The only exception to those plants enjoying constant clipping is the dwarf lavender, any unduly long shoots being cut back in spring rather than clipping in the normal way. When it is said that hedge plants require constant clipping, this does not mean more than once each year for most, and it should not be thought that a dwarf hedge will require a considerable amount of attention. Mostly, the hedge may be clipped when the beds are being tidied and replanted.

Soil, situation and size of garden or bed to be hedged, will play a part in the selection of the most suitable hedging plant. Where the beds are of miniature size, box, with its neat, glossy leaves or *Berberis dulsis nana* with its compact bottle-green foliage will prove most suitable. Where the garden is slightly larger, *Lonicera nitida* or *Santolina incana* will prove pleasing and efficient. The box and *berberis* may be allowed to grow no more than 6 in. tall, whilst the *Lonicera* and *Santolina* should be kept at a height of 10–12 in. Slightly taller growing are the rosemary and the lavender in their dwarf forms.

Extremely hardy and tolerant of sea winds is the *lonicera*, box, *santolina* and *olearia*, whilst the evergreen *ceanothus* and the dwarf *escallonias* prefer a warm, sheltered garden. Soil too should be considered. The slow growing variegated leaved holly and box like a heavy soil, whilst the *senecio*, *berberis* and lavender prefer a light, sandy soil. But whatever the choice may be, select a variety or species of compact, slow-growing habit and one that will withstand hard clipping. No plant which resents clipping should ever be used for a hedge however suitable it otherwise appears. Generally a plant which makes too much woody growth will resent hard clipping.

Where it is required to plant a hedge to divide one part of a small garden from another, then a more vigorous plant may be selected, and there are a number apart from the rather too vigorous privet and quick thorn, which will prove suitable, remaining neat and compact with the minimum of clipping. Here, the more vigorous *escallonias*, *Senecio Grayi* or *Thuya vervaeneana* will prove suitable.

As many of the dwarf hedging plants bear blossom in addition to their colourful foliage, exactly when to trim must be governed by the flowering time of the plant as well as by its susceptibility to frost damage, though plants growing in favourable districts will rarely be troubled by frost. Cutting back the hedge of the more tender plants in autumn may allow hard frost to penetrate the severed shoots thus causing them to die back after losing its top protection and the plant may succumb completely. Thus only the hardiest of plants should be trimmed in autumn unless it be that only occasional unduly long shoots require removing or shortening. It is important to keep the hedge trimmed from the beginning. To allow the plants to grow away and form an abundance of wood will not only cause them to become untidy, but when cut back they may take a considerable time to recover and regain their pleasing characteristics again.

These plants will make an attractive dwarf hedge.

(E. = Evergreen: D. = Deciduous.)

BERBERIS (E.). There are several charming species most suitable for edging, but none is daintier that *B. dulcis nana*, with its neat dark bottle-green foliage and bright orange-yellow flowers. Planted at 15 in. apart, the hedge may be kept at only 9 in. high, and is extremely tidy and neat. Another species, *B. Gagnepainei*, with its narrow olive-green leaves, may also be shaped into an attractive little hedge, likewise *B. Irwini*, with its dainty, arching branches and vivid orange flowers.

BOX (E.). There are two ways of spoiling a box hedge, one is to cut or trim at the wrong time of the year, another is to allow bedding plants to flop over the top, thus causing the attractive small, glossy green leaves to die back. In exposed gardens a box hedge may suffer frost damage if trimmed between September and March. Quite the best time to trim is June 1st, when the spring flowering plants are being replaced by those of summer flowering. The plants then have the summer months to heal and grow, and will be able to withstand the severest of weather without damage. When planting box, be sure it is the species *Buxus nana*, which is hardy and slow growing, and plant fifteen inches apart. Box grows best in a dry, sandy or gravelly soil, and where the soil is cold and heavy, some other dwarf plant should be used.

CYDONIA (D.). It is *C. Maulei*, the Chinese Dwarf Quince, which is suitable for a low hedge, whilst it is the most inexpensive of all the cydonias. It is of almost horizontal habit, and by removing the leader shoot when the plants are established, a hedge no taller than 12 in. may be formed, and which will require almost no attention. It will cover itself with delicate salmon shaded flowers in April, and bear equally attractive golden fruit in early autumn. Spur-back any long shoots in November. Plant 2 ft. apart.

ERICA (E.). Several of the heathers may be made to form an attractive low hedge for they withstand continued clipping which should be done each year early in summer, when flowering has generally ended. They prefer a lime-free soil though the Mediterranean heathers, so useful for a hedge, will thrive in any ordinary soil except perhaps over chalk. The winter and early spring flowering heaths will provide colour when there are few plants in bloom, whilst their dense bright green foliage accentuates the brilliance of colour of any summer bedding plants. One of the best for a low hedge is *E. darleyensis*, which produces its spikes of warm pink flowers from the New Year until April. Also lovely is Silver Mist, which bears its spikes of silvery white throughout mid-winter. Excellent too, is *E. scoparia nana,* which forms a rounded little bush of bright green and bears green flower spikes.

FUCHSIA (D.). Though most are quite hardy in the more favourable districts, only one or two varieties may be classed as being fully hardy in the more exposed areas. However, if all dead wood is allowed to remain on the plants until early May, when any pruning should be done, this will act as protection when the fuchsia will prove to be hardier than generally realized. Ashes heaped around the base of the plant in November should also help them to withstand a hard winter. For a very dwarf hedge which will be most charming during summer and autumn with its bell-like blooms, Tom Thumb planted 8 in. apart will be suitable; whilst for a slightly taller hedge, Mrs. Pople, bearing rose and violet blooms, and Dr. Foster, which bears a purple bloom with striking scarlet sepals will be most colourful.

HOLLY (E.). A most attractive little hedge may be formed with holly. Rooted cuttings only should be obtained and planted at an angle of 45°. When well established, the growing point should be removed so that the plants will be encouraged to form side shoots. In this way a low, bushy hedge of great durability may be formed within 2–3 years. Either Golden Queen or Silver King should be obtained for they are most colourful with their margined leaves and growth may not exceed 12 in.

LAVENDER (E.). Everybody loves a lavender hedge, not only for its richly perfumed flower spikes, but also for the silvery-green of its foliage. But the taller growing species and varieties, though famed for the amount of bloom they produce, are not suitable for a dwarf edging. Those that do remain dwarf and compact and make little unsightly wood are Hidcote Purple, with its rich violet blooms and bright silvery foliage and which is distinctly slow growing; Loddon Pink, a new introduction, the flower spikes being pale shell-pink; and Munstead, with its deep lavender coloured blooms. Each of these lavenders grows no taller than 15–16 in. and may be trimmed to remain even more dwarf. In dry districts and where the soil is dry and sandy, lavender will do well. For this reason it grows so well along the dry eastern coast of England. The best time to plant is in early spring, so that the plants may become well established before the frosts.

LONICERA (E.). Of the same family as the honeysuckle, it is the species *L. nitida* that is so valuable for surrounds. The more it is clipped the more dense it becomes, and with its glossy dark green leaves it is perhaps the best of all plants to use to edge a flower bed.

It is evergreen and quickly forms a low hedge, leaving no gaps. It should be planted in the autumn, whilst cutting is best performed at the end of April, and again in early August. The form, Baggesen's Gold is equally fine for a low hedge. Its leaves are brilliant gold in summer, changing to deep bronze in winter to give a most striking effect the whole year through.

OLEARIA Haasti (E.). A native of New Zealand and happy in the generally dry soil of a coastal garden. It forms a dwarf bush of box-like appearance, having glossy grey leaves and bearing clusters of white flowers during mid-summer. It withstands hard clipping and may be allowed to grow to any height between 8 in. and 2 ft. Plant 9 in. apart and trim early in spring. It has an advantage over most plants in that it quickly forms a dense hedge and is smoke tolerant.

OSMARA burkwoodii (E.). An evergreen with glossy dark green foliage, it makes a fine low hedge. It should not be clipped until early June, after it has flowered, for unpruned shoots are thickly set with clusters of fragrant white flowers which appear in April and May.

PITTOSPORUM mayii (E.). It should be confined to coastal gardens in the west for elsewhere this New Zealand shrub is not fully hardy. It has pale green glossy leaves waved at the edges, and black stems. It may be clipped in spring and kept into a small hedge if planted 2 ft. apart, or it may be allowed to grow tall when its long graceful shoots are cut for market.

POTENTILLA (D.). The shrubby *Potentillas* make most pleasing little hedges and will withstand any amount of cutting back which should be done early in spring. *P. beesii* has lovely silvery foliage and bears large golden geum-like flowers, whilst *P. jackmani* has almost blue-grey leaves and bears similar golden flowers. Slightly more vigorous is *P. veitchi* which has silvery green foliage and bears large pure white flowers. Plant in autumn, 12 in. apart and they like a well-drained soil containing some humus.

PYRACANTHA (E.). The Firethorns with their bright glossy dark green foliage and their shoots wreathed in winter berries are unrivalled for a dense low evergreen hedge. Plant 2 ft. apart. The two best forms are Orange Glow and Rogersiana, both of which bear brilliant orange berries.

RIBES alpinum aureum (D.). This member of the Flowering Currant family may be kept cut back to a height of 8–9 in. when it forms a delightful hedge though it is deciduous. Its leaves are golden-green, its tiny flower trusses being pale green and these are followed by scarlet berries. Plant in autumn 9 in. apart and cut back any long or straggling shoots at the same time.

SANTOLINA (E.). The species *S. incana* has small narrow leaves covered with silver-grey down, with pale greenish-yellow flowers borne during late summer. It has a neat, dwarf habit, and planted 15 in. apart and carefully trimmed, will soon form a dense hedge. It is especially attractive when the bed is filled with plants having bronzy-crimson foliage, or with plants that bear scarlet or crimson blooms. There is another dainty species which will make a low hedge, this is *S. alpina*, of tuft-like, shrubby habit which grows only 8 in. tall.

SENECIO Grayi compacta (E.). This is the best form for a dwarf hedge for it makes a low, dense bushy plant. It has dark grey-green leaves and bears yellow daisy-like flowers from June until October. It is quite slow growing and should be only lightly trimmed in autumn.

SYMPHORICARPOS (D.). Tough shrubs which are tolerant of all soils and are hardy enough for gardens of northern Europe and Canada. They make dense upright growth. Plant 18 in. apart and clip to the desired height. They make a valuable windbreak in exposed gardens. The variety White Hedge bears clusters of white fruits through winter and Magic Berry bears crimson berries in clusters of ten or more.

VERONICA (E.). The shrubby veronica withstand hard clipping and for a sea-coast garden there is no better plant for a low hedge. The varieties Autumn Glory and Bowle's Variety which bear clouds of violet flowers throughout summer and autumn are suitable for a hedge about 18 in. high. For a dwarf hedge, *V. pageana* with its attractive glossy grey leaves and white flower spikes and *V. hectori*, which has striking golden foliage though does not bloom are excellent plants. They should not be planted less than 15 in. apart and any clipping should be done early in autumn, the blooms appearing on the young shoots.

Chapter 10

CRAZY PAVING IN THE SMALL GARDEN

The value of paving – Laying the stone – paving plants.

THE use of crazy paving stone or of pre-cast concrete flagstones will be extremely attractive in the small garden, in addition to being labour saving, whilst in the town garden it remains untroubled by deposits of soot and sulphur which grass finds difficult to overcome. Correctly laid, paving is clean, weed free and enables one's hobby to be pursued during periods of wet weather when the frequent treading of grass would prove detrimental. Where a small garden is shaded, paving will also prove more satisfactory than grass, also where there are overhanging trees, dripping causing grass to die back owing to the roots becoming water-logged. In addition paving requires no upkeep, no laborious cutting and edging, so necessary with grass if the garden is to be kept tidy. Brushing and occasional swilling down is all that paving requires to maintain its cleanliness.

Paving may be used to surround a centre bed or lawn, for accommodating deck chairs beneath an ornamental tree, or it may be used to make a terrace or path. Miniature flower beds may be divided by small paths of crazy paving, using most ingenious designs or the entire area of a small garden may be covered with concrete flagstones. It should be said, however, that where prostrate plants are used about a paved path or yard, that bleak appearance of stone will be pleasantly softened, whilst a number of plants may be used that will provide colour almost the whole year round. There is nothing more attractive than paving which has been correctly laid and planted and though it may be necessary to consider the outlay, it will be permanent and require little or no attention.

Laying the Stone

To make a success of the laying of paving, some time and trouble should be taken. Paving badly laid will be difficult to walk upon, whilst the appearance of grass and weeds between the stones will become almost intolerable.

It may be said that crazy paving stone should be used for a small area or path, whilst for a larger area, such as a terrace, yard or roof garden, pre-cast concrete slabs are more satisfactory and more easily handled. It is a simple matter to measure up the area to be paved, and to ask one's supplier for stones to cover the necessary area. With concrete flagstones there is no need to spend time in endeavouring to fit them together so that the best use of the stone is made. Not only will the sides be cut quite straight but the stones will be exactly the same thickness. Before ordering the stones, first find out the various widths in which they can be supplied, then make your path or terrace of corresponding size, remembering that it is much easier to alter your ground measurements than to cut the stone. The stones being of the same size so that they will fit close up to each other, the need for a concrete bed is not so important, but as grass will eventually grow up through the slightest crack, concrete should be packed between each stone as it is placed into position. Be sure to make your base quite solid, either beating down the soil thoroughly or making the base of clinker or brick completely firm. This is particularly important when making a terrace surrounded either by a brick or stone wall, or by a rockery which may necessitate moving a considerable amount of soil before the base is formed. Subsiding of the soil will cause the stone to fall away and not only will the effect be spoilt but weeds will soon begin to appear through the cracks. As with crazy paving paths, pockets may be left at the corner of a number of stones to be filled with soil for carpeting plants. Into these pockets the excess rain water will drain, so that the terracing will rapidly dry out after even the most prolonged rain, which would make turf impossible to walk upon for some considerable time. Where the soil is of a clay nature it will be advisable to lay the stone on an inch of clinker or ash rolled quite firm so that excess moisture may more readily drain away.

When laying a path of crazy paving, first begin by marking out the necessary length and width, then remove several inches of soil depending on (a) the depth of stone, and (b) whether it is desired to lay the stone on to a thin bed of concrete.

The question of the concrete bed is all-important, for not only will it provide a firmer foundation which will prevent various stones from falling below the original level, which in time they so frequently do, but it will prevent the appearance of grass and weeds which are the curse of crazy paving. No matter how well the stone is laid, placing each stone tightly together with only the minimum of soil exposed, weeds will eventually push their way up from between the stones and will be almost impossible to clear. And there is no more irksome task in the garden than trying to clear a well-laid crazy paving path of grass and weeds. The concreting will be slightly more expensive in the first instance and will take more time to lay, but will be more than worth while. Pockets between the stones may be left free of concrete at irregular intervals, but do not overdo the plants, a few look much better than too many. The still wet concrete can be removed from the pockets after sections of the path are laid.

First select your stones before the work is to begin and if possible place them into something like order by the side of the path. Small stones may be placed into convenient heaps to be used to fill in any large gaps. A better job can be made of a terrace where either flags of crazy paving stone is being used if first a solid foundation of clinker or crushed brick or stone is made. This means taking out an extra 2–3 in. of soil, but a clinker foundation will make a much better base over which to place the concrete. Even where no concrete is being used on which to lay the stones, a clinker base will prove of untold value in providing additional drainage, especially if the path is at all low lying. The soil may be used to fill up the pocket, or better still, use a prepared compost.

Apart from a good spade, the only tool needed will be the important spirit level which will not only ensure a neater and more professional job, but will ensure that the stones are made level and so make for easier walking. Obtain a builder's "level", large enough to span across the path so that the top of the stone may be kept level with the sides of the ground. From the beginning of operations, make use of the "level", right from the time the clinker base is put down, for this will ensure that the concrete will also be level and will make the final laying of the stone a much easier matter. Be sure to have the flattest surface of the stone to the top, and of course, the sides should be kept as near straight as possible. A neat job can be done by laying (in cement) a row of bricks down each side of the path, placing them on their sides. The contrast in colour of brick and stone adds to the finished effect and will help to prevent the soil from falling on to the concrete as this is being placed into position, whilst it also makes the laying of the stone much easier. Remember to set the stones as close to each other as possible, for if too much concrete is used to point the path on completion, it will spoil the effect. If the stone can be laid close, no pointing needs to be done except to fill up those pockets into which it is not required to set a plant. My own method is to do the planting as the work proceeds. First make a satisfactory base which is quite level, then lay the stone in possibly 6 ft. lengths, completely finishing the stretch in every way before continuing with the next 6 ft. or so. Pockets for plants should have the concrete removed while still wet and this should either be filled up with compost and the plant set, or a small stick should be inserted to show the position for planting. All

Erythronium (Dog's Tooth Violet).
E. dens-canis album

The Spring Snowflake.
Leucojum vernum

Quaint hose-in-hose Primrose, Brimstone

The *Kaufmanniana* Tulip of dwarf habit

other pockets may then be filled with concrete and any pointing done before moving on to another stretch.

Paving Plants

They should be of creeping, prostrate habit.

ACAENA. Native of New Zealand and amongst the best of carpeting plants, the *acaenas* are evergreen of a pale green shade. The flowers produced in late summer being of almost the same colour. *A. Buchanani* is most attractive, whilst *A. macrophylla* is also a beauty, bearing little crimson burrs which are covered in prickles.

ANTENNARIA. Called the cat's ear and is one of the loveliest of all carpeting plants, the species *A. dioica rosea* producing tufts of silver-edged foliage with fluffy pink flowers which remains in bloom throughout summer. *A. dioica tomentosa* is equally attractive, with grey foliage and creamy-white flowers.

ARENARIA. Known as the Sandwort and a most valuable plant. The species *A. Baleorica* produces masses of tiny white flowers above a carpet of emerald green throughout early summer. Even lovelier is *A. caespitosa aurea,* which grows into tiny golden hummocks and looks most attractive with *A. Baleorica.* Then there is *A. tomentosa,* which has silver foliage. All of them may be trodden upon with freedom.

ARMERIA. Most of us know the thrift, symbolized on our threepenny piece coin, but it is the taller, *A. cephalotes,* that is most common. A lovely plant for carpeting is *A. caespitosa,* of dwarf habit and bearing tight green cushions studded with pink balls. Six Hills Variety from the old Six Hills Nursery, now alas no more, bears very large ball-shaped flowers.

AUBRETIA. Possibly the most popular of all plants for paving, for a rockery and for trailing over a wall. The Rock Cress must be given a sunny situation and a soil containing some humus. In bloom from April until mid-summer, it will quickly form a large clump and with its semi-trailing habit it should be kept in shape by the removal of any untidy shoots after it has flowered. Though plants may be raised from seed, the wonderful named varieties are propagated from short cuttings, taken after flowering and inserted round the sides of a pot, into a compost of peat and coarse sand. One of the finest varieties is Wanda, the blooms being of a brilliant red shade and produced over a longer period than those of any other aubretia. Another fine red is Russell's Crimson, which forms a plant of most compact habit. In the pale blue, Lancashire Beauty and Studland are outstanding, the blooms being large; whilst in purple shades, Magician and Wirral Purple bear large blooms of rich crimson-purple. There are now some lovely pink varieties, Lissadell Pink being a large rosy-pink bloom with an attractive white eye, whilst Maurice Prichard and Bressingham Pink bear bloom of a beautiful clear shell-pink, the latter bearing a fully double bloom.

CAMPANULA. There are a number suitable for paving. *C. Aucheri* producing its large violet bells in May; *C. garganica*, Blue Diamond, of similar prostrate habit following on with its deep blue star-like flowers; and *C. pulla lilacina*, producing its rosy bells above tiny green tufts, being three of the best. For a shady position, the *C. pusilla* hybrids are delightful.

COTULA. Amongst the most dwarf of all plants, *C. dioica* of creeping habit, makes a tiny carpet of brilliant green, the foliage being attractively serrated.

DRABA. Evergreen plants and bearing their yellow or white flowers during early summer, the drabas are splendid plants for a hot, dry position. Bearing its stemless little white flowers amidst a cushion of rich green is *D. dedeana*, of almost prostrate form. Of similar habit is *D. imbricata*, which smothers itself with bright yellow flowers from April until July.

EPILOBIUM nummularifolium. No plant has been blessed with a more awkward name, but in spite of it, it is an interesting carpeter. It has rich bronzy leaves, its tiny white flowers being followed by fluffy seed pods.

ERINUS. One of the loveliest plants for paving is *E. Dr. Hanele*, an evergreen of prostrate habit, which bears sprays of glowing carmine flowers during early summer. Equally lovely is another hybrid, Mrs. Charles Boyle, with its bloom of clear pink, both being enhanced by planting with the white form, *E. alpinus alba*.

GERANIUM. The species *G. Pylzowianum* is a superb paving plant rapidly spreading out and covering its stems in a mass of shrimp-pink flowers from May until September. It is a much too-refined plant to tread upon!

HOUSTONIA coerulea. A most charming little paving plant forming a tiny, compact tuft of bright green, covered throughout summer in a succession of brilliant blue starry flowers. The best form is Millard's Variety and it is happiest in a cool, semi-shaded position.

LINARIA. These dainty little plants are most attractive when planted between paving stones and so valuable is their prolonged period of flowering. Most dwarf is *L. aequitrilobia*, which bears masses of richest lavender flowers. Equally lovely is *L. alpina*, the deep violet flowers having a vivid orange spot on the lower lip, whilst the rosy-pink form, *L. alpina rosea*, is, in my opinion, one of the loveliest of all alpines.

LIPPIA repens. This is a most uncommon but easily grown alpine of creeping habit and bearing masses of mauve-pink flowers like those of scabious. The white form, *alba*, is equally lovely.

LITHOSPERMUM. This is a superb plant for paving, remaining in bloom from May until early autumn and forming a mat of pale green foliage covered with star-like bloom. The hybrid Grace Ward is of intense gentian-blue, whilst Heavenly Blue is of rich indigo-blue. Equally valuable for paving is *L. Oleifolium*, which forms neat grey-green tufts and clusters of rich blue flowers during early summer. Mix some peat around the roots at planting time.

LYSIMACHIA minuta. It is valuable because it is quite happy in full shade. It is a tiny creeper forming a rich green carpet and bearing small pale yellow flowers during July and August.

MAZUS rugosus. Happy in full sun or in semi-shade, this little-known plant is one of the hardiest and longest flowering of all. It is of trailing habit and from May until September is studded with lobelia-like flowers of mauve and gold.

MENTHA requieni. There is no lovelier carpeting plant, not so much for its beauty, but for the refreshing fragrance of its peppermint scented leaves, which give off the scent when trodden upon.

MORISIA hypogeae. Known as the Mediterranean Cress and happy in full sun or partial shade. It is an outstanding plant forming compact rosettes of bright green ferny foliage about which nestle, during March, April and May, stemless golden flowers.

PAROCHETUS. The vivid blue "Shamrock Pea" of trailing habit and in bloom during winter is an interesting plant, but must be planted only where the winter climate is kind, otherwise it is better in the alpine house.

PHLOX. For paving and for a sunny position plant the *Douglassii* hybrids of prostrate habit, whilst for shade plant *P. reptans*, of neat tufty habit and bearing brilliant lavender-blue flowers during early summer. In the *Douglassii* section, the plants forming emerald green carpets, Violet Queen bears purple-blue flowers; Eva bears lovely rose-pink flowers, whilst May Snow forms carpets of pure white and is well named.

POLYGONUM vaccinifolium. In spite of its name it is a most useful plant in that it is of compact, prostrate form and bears its tiny pink spikes throughout autumn when there will be few other paving plants in bloom.

RAOULIA. These tiniest of all alpines enjoy a moist root run and as little moisture on the foliage as possible and so are happiest planted amongst crazy paving. *R. australis*, with its silver foliage and fluffy pale yellow flowers, is charming, and so is the prostrate *R. lutescens*, with its grey foliage and golden flowers produced in autumn.

SAPONARIA. Happiest in full sun, *S. ocymoides rubra compacta* quickly forms a prostrate mat, covering itself through early summer with blooms of vivid crimson. To be long lived, it needs a well-drained soil.

SAXIFRAGE. Bearing neat, bright green mounds, the Mossy saxifrages are possibly the best for paving. They prefer a position of semi-shade and flourish under town garden conditions. They like a well-drained soil containing some grit. Very striking is Cloth of Gold which forms tight golden tuffets and bears pure white flowers. Plant with it Peter Pan which bears crimson flowers and has dark green foliage; or Pixie, of similar habit and colouring. Lovely too is Flowers of Sulphur with its pale yellow flowers and Cambria Jewel, with its bloom of rich pink.

SCLERANTHUS. A native of Tasmania it enjoys a position of full sun and though its tiny blooms are quite insignificant it is most attractive with its dainty hummocks of vivid golden foliage.

SEDUM. These are plants with an enormous range of species and varieties, almost all of them ideal for the paving garden. We know them as Stonecrop, at their best in full sun where their various tinted foliage shows to greatest advantage. The species *S. anopelatum glaucum*, with its silvery foliage, is most attractive, whilst Coral Carpet forms rich green clumps, turning bronze in autumn. *S. dasyphyllum*, prostrate, forms dainty glaucous green hummocks which turn rich mauve, whilst *S. lydium* turns from deep green to flaming scarlet. *S. hispanicum aureum* forms exquisite mats of gold and *S. oregonum* bronze rosettes with heads of orange. *S. Middendorfianum* is an interesting plant bearing golden flowers followed by scarlet seed pods, whilst *S. spathulifolium* forms rosettes of mealy grey leaves and vivid golden flowers.

THYMUS. "I know a bank where the wild thyme grows," wrote Shakespeare, and nowhere are these charming old-world plants happier than planted on a sunny bank or amidst crazy paving where they receive full sun. The foliage of all the thymes is richly aromatic, but none is more refreshing than the lemon fragrance of Lemon Curd, an almost prostrate thyme. *T. herba-barona*, which bears lilac flowers in June, has caraway-scented foliage, whilst *T. villosus*, which forms a mat of grey foliage, possesses the fragrance of verbena. But perhaps the most valuable of the thymes is *T. serpyllus* and its many hybrids and varieties, none of which grow more than 1 in. tall with *serpyllus minus* even more dwarf. Outstanding is *T. serpyllus coccineus*, which bears masses of rich crimson flowers, and with it plant the white counterpart, *albus*. Really lovely is the new Pink Chintz, which covers itself with flowers of a pretty shade of salmon.

Chapter 11

GARDENING IN TUBS

The wide use of a garden tub – Preparation of the tub – Plants suitable for tub culture – Trees in tubs – Fruit in tubs – Tubs for a water garden.

WHERE there is no garden, possibly only a veranda or terrace, a flat roof or a small back yard, tubs can be made to play a part in the fulfilment of one's desires to have a garden however small. Indeed, with its depth of soil, considerably more may be done with a tub than with a window box. Those plants requiring a larger supply of moisture about their roots may be grown in a tub and those requiring a considerable depth of soil. Cordon and horizontally-trained apples and pears may be grown in tubs around a sunny courtyard, also most of the popular soft fruits, including the strawberry and tomato. Tubs may also be used for a climbing plant, a clematis or rose which may be trained about the wall of a house or yard, whilst almost all plants, from the miniatures to the taller growing trees and shrubs will be quite happy in a well-prepared tub.

The size of the tubs and the height of the plants will be governed by the size of the yard, roof or terrace, but the most attractive display may be obtained from a tub which has a fairly wide diameter and is not too tall. Those most conforming to these dimensions are the cider casks, obtainable from the Barrel House, St. Agnes, Cornwall and though they will have been used in the storing of cider they will give many more years service in the growing of plants. The casks which will have been sawn in two will be of seasoned oak and will not require treating in any way, though they may be painted on the outside if a more colourful effect is required. They will look more attractive where placed against the colour washed walls of house or yard. Treat the iron rims with a rust-proof paint.

One of the most attractive town gardens that I know is composed of a tiny courtyard paved with concrete flagstones, between which plants of thyme were growing. Around the washed walls tubs had been arranged and were planted with all manner of summer flowering plants including those of trailing habit which almost clothed the sides of the tubs. A few moments attention each week with watering and the removal of dead blooms is all that is necessary. After the summer display has ended, the tubs are cleared, the soil refortified with a little peat or hope manure, and then replanted with bulbs and spring flowering plants, whilst winter flowering pansies, primroses and *Erysimum linifolius* provide colour through the darkest days of winter.

Preparation of the Tub

To enable the plants to take advantage of the greater depth of soil, the tubs must receive just the same thorough preparation as given the window box. In the same way, holes should be drilled at the base, over which is placed a layer of crocks or broken brick to a depth of 2 in., so that in the event of wet weather, ample drainage is available. Over the crocks should be placed partially rotted turves and a layer of decayed stable manure. This should just about fill up half the tub. The balance will be of prepared compost, depending much upon the requirements of the plants that are to occupy the tubs. Dahlias, for instance, prefer a soil liberally enriched with decayed manure and peat, whereas geraniums, though having a liking for a little rotten manure, prefer a soil which is drier and contains less humus. As a general rule, the compost should consist of new turf loam, the soil of town gardens which is frequently inert and extremely acid being quite unsuitable. As the compost should be left in the tubs for several years, it goes without saying that it should be well prepared. Kettering loam is excellent where it can be obtained, but loam from pasture land which will be fibrous and free from weed spores will be equally as valuable. Mix with it some well-decayed manure, preferably cow manure or a quantity of used hops. Peat is also excellent, especially where the soil is of a heavy nature. A well prepared soil will not only produce a healthy and free flowering plant but will ensure that the plants do not suffer from lack of moisture at the roots. This will enable the tubs to be left for several weeks at a time without the plants coming to any great harm. Also, being in a more open situation than a window box, the plants will be better able to take up more natural moisture by way of dew and rain.

Before filling, the tub should be raised on pieces of wood or crazy paving stone of no more than 1 in. thickness and should be made quite secure so that the tubs cannot tilt. This will greatly prolong the life of the tubs by keeping the base above ground level, providing a circulation of air and preventing the tubs remaining for long periods in pools of rain water.

After the tubs have been filled to the brim with the prepared compost, allow it a full week in which to settle down before planting. This it will do, leaving about 2 in. from the soil level to the top of the tub to allow for watering and for a top dressing to be given where necessary. It will also prevent water from being splashed over the sides by heavy rain.

To prevent the soil from becoming sour, it should be given a top dressing with lime each year when cleared of the summer flowering plants. This, together with the careful preparation of the soil, should give the compost a life of at least four years before refilling is necessary.

It should be said that where the tubs are situated in a shaded position, only those plants which are tolerant of shade should be grown. Plants growing to a height of from 6–20 in. will be suitable for a tub though much will depend upon its size and situation.

Plants Suitable for Tub Culture

ASTILBE. These are excellent plants for a tub in a sunless position, where, so long as they are given a compost containing plenty of peat to ensure retention of moisture during summer, the plants will require little or no attention. The soil of the tub should not be limed. The plants will be permanent and if several varieties are planted together a long succession of bloom may be enjoyed.

Coming into bloom in early June, the snow-white Irrlicht and the crimson Gertrude Brix are outstanding when planted together. Two which bear a bloom of soft clear pink are Erica and Gloria. The new Red Sentinel and the bright rose-red Federsee bloom in July. To flower during August, Venus, flesh-pink; Jo Orphorst, ruby-red; and Fire, salmon-red, are all excellent. With this plant it is noticeable that the later varieties grow slightly taller than those which bloom first.

BEGONIA. Besides the multiflora types described in Chapter 4, the large flowered tuberous begonia is an excellent plant for tub culture, the tubers being started into growth in gentle heat in the early spring so that they have formed one or more leaves by the time they are planted out early in June. Tubers of mixed varieties and colours may be inexpensively obtained for this purpose and will give a rich and trouble-free display though they will require more summer moisture than will geraniums.

CALCEOLARIA. On account of the rich colouring of its blooms which are continuously borne until autumn, this is an excellent plant used with salvias or scarlet geraniums. Golden Gem and Bronze Beauty are the two best calceolarias for tub culture.

The best time to take cuttings is in September, and only those shoots which have not borne a flower should be removed. Firm side shoots should be selected and these should be inserted into boxes containing a mixture of peat and sand. If kept in a temperature of 60° F. they will root in several weeks, but take longer to root than most plants, for the shoots are hard and shrub-like. Early in spring, when well rooted, the plants should be transferred to 3-in. pots containing the same materials as for salvias, and from then onwards should be given the same treatment. As the cuttings show a tendency to damp off, powdered charcoal should be scattered over the compost, and they should be kept dusted with sulphur whilst rooting.

DAHLIA. Several of the modern dwarf bedding varieties, making bushy plants about 18–20 in. in height are excellent for tub culture. They like a soil containing plenty of humus, for they are gross feeders. The tubers may be wintered in boxes of peat or sand in a frost-free shed or room, and where there is no greenhouse, may be brought into growth in a sunny room by planting in boxes of soil and peat. So that there will be as little delay as possible in the plants coming into bloom, the tubers should be started into growth before planting out early in June after the wallflowers and tulips have finished blooming.

Most striking are the new Zulu Hybrids, the bloom being of rich deep colouring, the foliage almost a black-green. Excellent, too, is the yellow cactus-flowered variety Downham, and the double crimson-scarlet Pride of Edentown. Also most valuable, is Jescot Gloria with bronzed foliage and golden-yellow flowers; and Rothesay Castle, the fully double blooms being of a rich shade of cream overlaid rose-pink.

FUCHSIA. The hardier varieties make most charming tub plants and given the shelter of a wall and a straw or bracken covering around the crowns during winter, a far greater number may be grown this way than in the more exposed open ground. The plants may occupy the tubs for many years and will greatly benefit from a dressing of peat and decayed cow manure each year when they finish flowering. They will also appreciate a fortnightly application of diluted manure water which will greatly prolong the season, often until Christmas in a sheltered garden. The plants are copious drinkers when in tubs and if dry conditions continue the plants should be given a thorough soaking whenever the soil requires it from mid-April until the end of summer.

GERANIUM. This is an excellent tub plant, all members of this large family described in Chapter 4 being ideal as well as a number of others having a rather more vigorous habit. A most pleasing display may be obtained by planting to the centre of a tub the trailing variegated leaved L'Elegante and training the shoots up small canes. This should be surrounded with bedding geraniums and around the sides of the tub should be planted either the most dwarf varieties such as Black Vesuvius or the trailing ivy-leaved varieties, particularly fine being Mrs. W. A. R. Clifton with its vivid green foliage and double rose-bud flowers of vermilion-scarlet. Or plant at the centre the lemon-scented *P. crispum variegatum* of spire-like habit and with its attractively crinkled leaves of deep green, edged with gold. Surround with variegated leaved varieties of compact habit and edge with trailing lobelia, Sapphire.

HYDRANGEA. Excellent for permanent planting in tubs and completely labour-saving in that once planted, apart from the removal of dead blooms after flowering and of any dead wood in April, the plants will require almost no attention. The hydrangea is hardy in all parts of Britain, planting being done early in April into a soil containing peat and plenty of decayed manure. Blue flowers may be obtained by watering with aluminium sulphate, 2 oz. dissolved in a gallon of water. The pink colouring may be accentuated by working in mortar rubble around the roots at planting time. Excellent varieties which will not be too vigorous are:

HELGE. Mid-season and bearing, after aluminium sulphate treatment, a huge deep blue flower. Of dwarf bedding habit.

MADAME MOULLIERE. Very early and in all soils bears a huge pure white bloom of perfect form.

MISS BELGIUM. Very early flowering, the bloom with treatment being a deep violet colour or a crimson-red where no treatment is given.

PARSIVAL. The huge bloom is a deep carmine shade, with attractive serrated petals. It is dwarf and early to bloom. When treated the colour is an almost purple-red.

MARGUERITE. Because of their rather informal habit, they were at one time planted with geraniums and calceolarias; their whiteness, long-lasting qualities, and their ability to flourish under all conditions, made them a perfect foil for the brilliant colours and stiff habit of their neighbours. The plant may be classed as almost hardy, yet to propagate, the cuttings should be struck in gentle heat. October is the best time to remove the shoots from the leaf joints, when the plants are being removed from the beds. They are inserted in a compost of loam, peat and sand and kept in a temperature of 55° F., spraying occasionally to prevent flagging. As soon as rooted, the plants should be potted into 3-in. pots in a compost containing some decayed manure and some grit. Like the geranium, the plants should be given very little water until the sun's rays stimulate growth towards the end of March. During April, as with all these half-hardy plants, heat will only be necessary at night; and from May 1st not at all. Early in May the plants should be moved to cold frames and hardened-off in the normal way for planting in the tub early in June.

SALVIA. Whilst Scarlet Pigmy is the best variety for miniature bedding, those growing to a height of 12–14 in. are more suitable for tub culture. Excellent varieties are Harbinger, vivid scarlet; and Blaze of Fire, crimson-red. They are increased from cuttings taken in early autumn and rooted round the sides of a pot in a temperature of 55° F. As soon as rooted the plants should be transferred to small pots to be grown on through winter and spring in a temperature of 50° F. A stiff loam to which has been incorporated a little decayed manure and some grit will suit them well and though the plants will require little water during the winter months, they will need copious amounts as the sun gathers strength. Plant out early in June after hardening, six plants to a tub and surrounded with white lobelia, ageratum or alyssum for contrast, and which makes a striking display long in bloom.

Besides these plants which are so valuable for tub culture, the dwarf roses, Lilliput chrysanthemums and a number of hardy border plants such as the dwarf michaelmas daisies, in addition to the spring flowering plants, i.e. wallflowers and polyanthuses will be suitable subjects for tubs and these have been described in previous chapters. Most annuals too, will flourish in a tub and apart from those of dwarf habit described in Chapter 3, the taller flowering antirrhinums, godetias, calendulas, asters and stocks may all be grown, indeed almost any variety of reasonably compact habit.

Bulbs for Tub Culture

Not only are some of the miniature bulbs quite charming in tubs, some of those which are stronger growing may also be used:

AGAPANTHUS. This, the Blue African Lily, is a valuable bulbous plant for tub culture, *A. umbellatus* being the hardiest species, bearing its blue lily-like flowers during July and August. The pure white form, *alba*, is just as lovely. The plants prefer a soil containing plenty of peat or leaf mould and they like a sunny but sheltered position, such as provided by a sunny courtyard. If in any way exposed, the tubs should be removed to the shelter of a wall during winter. Only where the roots have become really tub-bound will the agapanthus bloom profusely, so prepare the soil thoroughly before planting and do not disturb for several years.

AMARYLLIS Belladonna. Not quite completely hardy except in the most favourable districts, the Belladonna lily requires similar conditions to the agapanthus, a soil containing plenty of humus and a sunny though sheltered position. If growing in the less favourable districts, the tubs should be removed to the protection of a shed or cellar, for the plants do not like root disturbance when once established. Plant the bulbs 6 in. deep. From mid-August to early October the lovely pink nodding lily-like blooms are borne on leafless stems above green strap-like foliage.

HYACINTH. All the large flowering varieties may be used for tub culture, the bulbs being planted in autumn. A most pleasing display which will take away much of their stiffness of habit will be to plant double daisies or the most dwarf of the Juliae primroses as a ground cover, also around the side of the tub. With hyacinth Blue Danube, the salmon-pink double daisy, Bellis Dresden China, is extremely pleasing; or with hyacinth, Queen of the Whites, plant double daisy, Rob Roy, or primrose, Hillhouse Red, with its bronzy-red foliage and crimson-red bloom.

LILY. All those lilies which do not grow too tall will be suitable for tub culture. If several are planted together, selecting those which are either lovers or haters of lime so that they may be given the most suitable conditions, there will be a continuous display right through summer and autumn.

These varieties grow best in a soil which is free of lime:

L. pyrenaicum	May
L. tenuifolium	May
L. Hansonii	June
L. regale	July
L. amabile	August
L. tigrinum	September

Each of these lilies have also another common characteristic, that is they are all stem rooting. They should, therefore, be planted 6 in. deep for they form roots at the base of the stem in addition to the base of the bulb. They will also appreciate a top dressing when forming their buds, using a mixture of peat or leaf mould and soil.

To the above list should be added the wonderful *L. candidum*, the Madonna Lily. It flowers in June and is not only a lover of lime, indeed it grows badly without it, but it is base rooting. It should, therefore, be grown on its own when it makes a fine tub plant. Plant the bulbs 3 in. deep and do not disturb for years. Allow it to die down gradually and if the tub is edged with annuals, the display will be continued through summer and autumn.

TULIP. No flower is more attractive grown in tubs than the tulip and besides the dwarf single and double early tulips, those of the Darwin and Cottage tulips, and the Triumphs with their exotic colour combinations are equally suitable. The taller varieties such as Chappaqua and Zina for instance, which reach a height of 30 in., should not be included but there is a wide selection to bloom at a height of between 12–24 in. Lovely together are Darwin tulips,

Charles Needham with its huge blood-red bloom held on 24-in. stems, and Cottage tulip, Carrara which bears a solid pure white bloom on 20-in. stems. Plant six bulbs of each to a tub and edge with red and white double daisies which will be in bloom at the same time.

Trees in Tubs

Oak tubs having a diameter and depth of about 15 in. and containers made of concrete "bricks" of similar dimensions will provide an attractive and satisfactory container for conifers and flowering shrubs of compact habit, also for box and yew trained to various designs. Evergreen box cut to ball shape or as a square and held on stems 2–3 ft. in length, or trained into pyramidal form or into the shape of animals or birds may be obtained from specialist growers. Being slow growing box and yew will require the minimum of clipping, a small pair of shears being used to maintain the shape by trimming which is best done early in summer. Conifers and shrubs of compact habit and flowering trees such as the laburnum and flowering cherry may be kept in bounds by the removal of unduly long shoots.

Trees and shrubs like a stiff, loamy soil containing a little decayed manure and some coarse sand to maintain drainage. The tubs will be prepared exactly as already described, and should be stood on stones or wooden blocks to prevent drainage holes in the base from becoming choked. Trees demand firm planting, the soil being pressed down well around the roots, having first ensured that the tubs are well provided with drainage materials. The plants will derive great benefit from a yearly top dressing of fresh loam and decayed manure, so it is advisable to allow, when planting, 2 in. from the top of the soil to the top of the tub, the space being gradually filled up through the years.

Trees and shrubs used in this way may be placed around a courtyard, about the wall of a raised terrace, on a flat roof, or may be used to hide the ugly wall of a house or outbuilding, two or three transforming the most unpleasant looking part of the property and with a little attention the trees will be just as satisfactory as where growing in the open ground.

Fruit in Tubs

In addition to cordon apples and horizontally trained pears which will bear heavy crops when grown in tubs, both strawberries and tomatoes, especially the dwarf varieties, The Atom and Amateur will provide a continuous supply of fruit from early summer until autumn, occupying a few square feet of ground. They must, however, be given a sunny situation in which to ripen their fruit, though strawberries will be happy in partial shade.

STRAWBERRIES. Though it will not accommodate as many plants, a tub or half barrel is more satisfactory for strawberries than is a full barrel, which is more frequently used for their culture. A tub will allow more moisture to reach those plants growing low down the sides than is possible with a barrel.

The tub should first be drilled at the base with drainage holes, then round the side, the holes to take the plants being made of 1 in. diameter. The plants are best inserted with their roots in the compost as the tub is filled. As strawberries prefer a slightly acid soil, peat should be used in quantity after first making it thoroughly moist. The soil should be of a fibrous turf loam, to which is added

the peat and some decayed manure or used hops. The addition of liberal amounts of humus will, apart from the manurial value, provide the plants with the moisture they require, so necessary for them to bear large, juicy fruits. Should May be a dry month, which it so often is, give the tub a thorough soaking so that the moisture is able to penetrate to those plants growing near the bottom of the tub. A weekly application of liquid manure water given whilst the fruit is swelling will enhance the quality.

So that there will be fruit throughout summer and autumn, plant several varieties. For very early fruit Cambridge Vigour, a very heavy cropper is excellent. To follow, the well-known Royal Sovereign is difficult to better, whilst slightly later to ripen its fruit is the new Talisman which bears the same attractive wedge-shaped berry which is of similar quality. Later still, is Cambridge Rearguard, whilst to continue fruiting until almost Christmas, plant the perpetual fruiting variety, La Sans Rivale.

As many as a dozen plants may be planted at the top of a tub, and two dozen round the sides. Planting is best done in early autumn so that the plants may settle in and form new roots before winter.

Tubs for a Water Garden

Where space is restricted and capital limited, a tub may be made into a most pleasing water garden, to be used as a centre piece and surrounded by crazy paving, or grass, or it may be placed in a corner of a garden. It will be necessary to obtain a tub which is quite water-tight and it may be inserted to its rim in the ground, or placed on a balcony or roof garden or a courtyard and planted just as it is. Possibly a tub inserted in the ground will be more attractive and if the rim is allowed to protrude 1 in. above soil level, crazy paving may be placed around the tub to a width of about 2 ft. The stone should be set in a layer of cement to prevent weeds from becoming a nuisance as described for laying a concrete path. It will be found that when the tub is filled with water, the staves will swell and provided a sound tub is obtained there should be no leakage. But before filling with water, the tub must be planted.

No pool, however small, will be complete without its water lily and one of the charming miniatures should be chosen. Lovely is *Nymphaea pygmaea alba*, with its dainty pure white flower, but even lovelier is *N. p. helvola*, which bears a bloom of primrose-yellow. To plant, a 3-in. thick layer of soil should be placed at the bottom of the tub and pressed well down and into this the roots are planted. Around the sides of the tub, which will be 12–15 in. deep, should be placed stones to a depth of 6–7 in., in the pockets of which soil is pressed. It is here that the marginal or water-side plants are set for they do not like more than 6–7 in. of water over their roots. Between the stones are planted two or three oxygenating plants to maintain purity of the water and three to four marginal plants to add to the charm of the pool and lend a more natural appearance. The dwarf bullrush, *Typha minima*, is most attractive and there are several lovely water irises amongst which is *I. laevigata* which has slender grass-like leaves and bears its lovely blue flowers during July and August (Rose Queen bears lilac-pink flowers); and *I. siberica* which bears its flowers on stiff stems 2–3 ft. long. Eric the Red bears wine-red flowers and Perry's Blue, blooms of sky-blue.

Plants may be obtained from specialist growers in June, for this is the most suitable time to make up a miniature pool. At first the water will appear muddy but will soon clear and should remain so, though soil and other material should not be thrown in. The water lily will bloom from early June until well into October and will be the centre of admiration.

Chapter 12

THE TROUGH GARDEN

Construction of a trough – Making up the trough – Plants for a trough – Miniature trees and shrubs.

WHERE space is strictly limited, the pleasures of the garden, with its trees and shrubs and plants in miniature may be enjoyed by making a trough garden. Placed around the walls of a house or courtyard, on a veranda, terrace or roof, or about a paved garden, a trough, whether it be of concrete or old stone will present a most attractive appearance and provide colour and interest throughout the year in return for the minimum of attention. Though there is nothing quite comparable to weathered stone, plants will grow equally well in a sink provided the surface is made rough, or in a concrete trough which will have one great advantage in that it will be porous, thus keeping the soil sweet and the roots healthy.

Of whatever material the trough is to be constructed, it should be provided with a drainage hole and will be more efficient and more easily managed if raised on a suitable base 3 ft. from the ground. If the trough is to be of concrete then the base should be built of breeze blocks. These blocks may also have crushed stone incorporated which will give them the appearance of stone and will thus also be suitable for a base for an old stone trough. A sink may be supported on rustic bricks to good effect, especially where it is to be used against the walls of a newly-built house of the same material.

It is important to ensure that the trough is not placed where rain water may drip on to the plants and so tend to wash them out of the soil. Unless the eaves of the house are wide, then the trough is best placed about 2 ft. from the wall. Also, the trough should not be placed beneath overhanging trees, from which melting snow and rain will drip almost continuously through the winter months.

Construction of a Trough

The most satisfactory way of constructing a concrete trough is to make two boxes of matured timber, making one about 1½ in. smaller in all dimensions. The smaller box will fit inside the other. For the base and walls of the trough mix up 2 parts of sand to 1 part of cement, adding sufficient water to make it into a paste so that it will "pour", yet at the same time it must not be too "sloppy". The cement

The Alpine Allwoodii on a rockery

Mushrooms in boxes
(*Above*) Inserting the spawn in the compost
(*Left*) First flush of Mushrooms from the same box

should be poured inside the first box to a depth of $1\frac{1}{2}$ in., two large corks being held in position to provide the drainage holes. To reinforce the base and sides, a length of wire netting should be pressed into the cement mixture just before it begins to set and this should extend almost to the top of the sides. A second piece of netting should be pressed into the mixture so that it extends up the other two sides in a similar way. Use 2-in. mesh netting, cutting the pieces to the exact measurements of the mould. Thus for a box 30 in. long × 18 in. wide × 6 in. deep, the two pieces of netting will measure 42 in. and 30 in. The smaller box does not require a base, just make the four sides and hold them together by small pieces of wood nailed across each corner and long enough to stretch across the corners of the first box to prevent it pressing into the concrete base. The cement is then poured between the two boxes. Insert a piece of stick to hold the netting away from the mould and this will prevent it showing when the concrete has finally set hard, which it will do in about twenty-four hours if not made too thin. Just before the cement has set completely, the sides of the boxes are carefully removed, the inner mould being left in position until thoroughly hardened. The wooden base and the corks are then pressed off.

A glazed sink which is to be used for a trough garden should be chipped as much as possible so that the sink will be more porous, and the roots of the plants will be able to hug the sides in the same way as do plants in earthenware pots. For the same reason plants growing in old stone and concrete troughs have a vigorous root action and as a result, top growth is equally vigorous and healthy.

Making Up the Trough

Troughs are extremely heavy, of whatever material they are constructed, so should be given a position of permanency before they are prepared for the plants. Make certain that they are quite firm on a single or double pedestal, using wedges where necessary. Over the drainage holes place several large crocks, or pieces of brick or stone, then over the base place a layer of small stones or crocks to a depth of 6 in. Over this lay old turves upside down and then fill to the top with the prepared compost, pressing it well down round the sides. This should be composed of:

- 2 parts fresh loam, sterilized if possible
- 1 part top grade peat, which is superior to leaf mould because it contains no weed spores
- 1 part coarse sand and grit.

Add a sprinkling of superphosphate to encourage root action, and lime to keep it sweet; also a little bone meal, a slow-acting fertilizer, and mix the whole together. If one has no garden, sterilized loam, peat and sand may readily be obtained from a local nursery and as a general guide, a barrowful of compost will be required for a sink of approximately 36 in. × 18 in. × 6 in. Most stone troughs are several inches deeper, but rarely more than 24–26 in. in length, so that compost requirements will be much the same. Some troughs have no drainage holes and so should be given a greater depth of drainage material, whilst some pieces of broken charcoal should be mixed with the compost to maintain its sweetness.

So many ways of making up a trough or sink are available that there is something for every taste. The troughs may be used in much the same way as window boxes or tubs, planting them with spring flowering plants such as primroses and winter flowering pansies to be followed by multiflora begonias, ivy-leaf geraniums or suitable annuals such as verbena and *Phlox Drummondii*. However, it is as a more permanent garden that the sink or trough is most suitable. The dwarf roses may be used by themselves to make a miniature rose garden, using possibly four different varieties and dividing them by tiny paths of stone. Or the trough or sink may be made into a miniature rockery, complete with weathered stone, dwarf conifers or shrubs and tiny perennial plants to provide colour all the year round. The smallest of the miniature bulbs may also be used, the whole so laid out as to give a completely natural appearance.

When planting, care must be taken in selecting the most suitable plants for certain soil conditions and situations. Plants requiring a soil containing plenty of lime, such as the fragrant little *Iris reticulata*, and the alpine pinks should be given some lime rubble in the compost, and the lime lovers should be planted together. Those which are lime haters must also be kept together. There are plants which prefer shade, others a position of full sun. Only the really hardy plants should be used, for the range is large enough to satisfy all tastes, and the less hardy plants may fail to come up to expectations if the winter is unduly wet or cold.

Where possible use plants from small pots so that root disturbance is at a minimum. Planting may be done at almost any time of the year, though autumn and spring would seem to be the most suitable periods. However, before planting allow the soil time to settle down so that there are no air pockets and when making a miniature rockery, place in several stones, grouping them as naturally as possible. Tufa stone from the hills of Derbyshire and Westmorland is the most suitable, but weathered red sandstone or Cotswold stone is almost as good. Set the stone well into the soil so that the plants may send down their roots into the moisture, almost always to be found around those portions of the stone which are under soil level. Placing the stones well into the soil will also prevent them from being moved when the trough is receiving attention, for established plants will occasionally be replaced with those which may be considered more attractive, whilst others will need trimming to keep them in bounds. The soil will also require stirring to prevent it "panning", whilst all weeds must be removed immediately they are noticed. The soil should never be allowed to dry out during the summer months.

The best effect will be obtained from the trough and sink garden by grouping the plants as naturally as possible. Plant one or two conifers together, with two or three primulas around a stone, with possibly a miniature shrub to give partial shade to the primulas, so building up the garden in such a way that the plants will fit into the scheme just as if nature herself had done the planting.

Plants for the Trough Garden

A suitable plant for a trough or sink must be long flowering and have a most compact habit. Almost all those miniature bulbs mentioned in Chapter 7 will be suitable and should be planted in groups of three between the flowering plants and miniature trees. Care should be taken with the selection of varieties so that there will be colour over a long period rather than a large flush at any one time followed by long colourless periods. Those plants of semi-trailing habit should be planted along the sides of the trough. Elsewhere, only those plants should be used which have a tufted or upright habit.

Plants for a Trough

AETHIONEMA Mavis Holmes. This is a tiny, stiff, glaucous-green shrublet, which bears large rose-pink blooms from May till late in July. It grows to a height of only 4 in.

ANDROSACE. The Rock Jasmines are amongst the best plants for a trough garden, *A. sarmentosa Watkinsii* bearing umbels of rich crimson blooms held on 4-in. stems above woolly rosettes. *A. lanuginosa* bears clusters of crimson flowers with a striking golden eye. They enjoy full sun.

ANTENNARIA dioica rosea. Above the interesting silver-edged foliage the dainty fluffy pink flowers are borne on 3-in. stems.

ARMERIA caespitosa. Its tight rich green tuffets are studded with pink ball-shaped flowers during May and June. Bevan's Variety bears large globes of deepest pink.

ARTEMESIA glacialis. A lovely shrublet for growing near the dark evergreens, for it is of most compact habit and has attractive silvery foliage.

ASPERULA Gussoni. It forms tiny grey tufts and throughout summer covers itself with minute pink trumpets. It likes a gritty soil and a position of full sun.

AUBRETIA. Indispensable plants for trailing over the sides of a trough. Of almost prostrate habit, their blooms, about the size of a sixpenny piece, are borne in profusion during spring and early summer. Outstanding is Kelmscott Beauty, double dusky-pink; Studland, light blue; Godstone, deep purple; and the rich crimson, Barker's Double.

BELLIS. Quite the most attractive Double Daisy for a sink is Dresden China, with its tiny double blooms of a lovely shade of shell-pink borne on 3-in. stems.

BERBERIS corallina compacta. This tiny evergreen bears sprays of orange flowers during May whilst its glossy leaves remain attractive throughout the year.

BRYANTHUS. This prostrate shrub of the heather family requires a peaty soil and partial shade. During early summer it bears clusters of vivid pink heath-like flowers.

CALCEOLARIA Darwinii. A most interesting plant bearing its huge yellow "slippers" on only 2-in. stems. The blooms are splashed with brown and have a strange white band across.

CAMPANULA. There are dozens of members of this huge family which will prove suitable for sinks. For trailing over the sides none is lovelier than the hybrid E. H. Frost, with its pure white wax-like flowers. Another hybrid bearing deep violet bells on short, erect stems, is the new *C. Covadonga*; whilst for a semi-shaded position *C. pusilla alba*, like a tiny white harebell and its blue companion, Oakington Blue, remain in bloom from June until October.

CASSIOPE lycopodioides. A shrublet of the heather family requiring a peaty soil. Of almost prostrate habit it has dark green foliage and bears dainty white bells, like lily-of-the-valley blooms.

CERASTIUM alpinum. This is not the common trailing form but a tufted miniature which has silver foliage and bears grey-white flowers through summer. Lovely as a foil to darker foliaged plants it grows only 2 in. tall.

CRASSULA sediformis. It likes a gritty soil and full sun and forms tiny bronze-green cushions, covered throughout summer with pinky-white flowers.

CYANANTHUS integer. A glorious plant, growing no taller than 2 in., and which bears its powder-blue bells on slender trailing stems through summer and autumn.

DIANTHUS. The neat Rock Pinks with their tufts of blue-grey foliage are ideal plants for a trough garden, but they do like some lime in the soil. A lovely variety is Anne, which bears tiny double blooms of cerise-pink; whilst equally charming is Elizabeth, its double pink flowers having an attractive brown centre. But for a real splash of colour, Fusilier and Bombardier, both bearing bright scarlet bloom right through summer, are outstanding.

ERIGERON. Several species of the Flea Bane are ideal for a small rockery or trough, *E. alpinus* is of tufted habit and bears deep pink daisy-like flowers during early summer, whilst *E. leiomerus* bears little mauve daisies on 2-in. stems from May until October.

ERODIUM corsicum. It forms attractive grey-green tufts and throughout summer bears masses of pretty pink-veined, bell-shaped flowers.

ERYTHRAEA Chloodes. A member of the gentian family and a lovely plant for a sunny position. It grows only 2 in. tall and from June until October bears its beautiful shell-pink trumpets.

GEUM montanum. An interesting plant bearing throughout summer, yellow stemless flowers followed by attractive, fluffy seed pods.

GLOBULARIA pygmaea. The Globe Daisy, which enjoys a position of full sun where it will produce its mauve daisy-like flowers during mid-summer.

HELIANTHEMUM. The lovely shrubby rock roses are mostly rather too large for a trough or small rockery, for they form bushy plants 7–8 in. tall and a similar width. Two, however, are suitable, Ben Mare grows only 4–5 in. tall and bears large blooms of clear orange, whilst *H. alpestre* is even more compact and bears brilliant yellow flowers throughout summer.

HYSSOPUS aristatus. It forms a neat, upright shrublet less than 6 in. tall and throughout summer bears tiny spikes of bright blue.

IBERIS Jordani. This little Candytuft forms a cluster of dark green leaves covered in flat, white flowers during June.

LYCHNIS alpina. Valuable in that it bears its pretty spikes of rosy-pink from mid-April until June, when few plants are in bloom.

MIMULUS. Though most are rather too vigorous for a trough, *M. primuloides* grows only 2–3 in. tall and bears its dainty pale yellow tubes throughout summer over a carpet of emerald green.

MORISIA hypogaea. From March until June it bears its stemless golden flowers above rosettes of bright green ferny leaves and is quite happy in partial shade.

MYOSOTIS explanata. Around its tuffets of bristly leaves it bears its stemless white star-like flowers in mid-summer.

NIEREMBERGIA rivularis. Known as the Cup Flower and a

lovely plant, forming a mat of dark green on which sit large white cups. It likes moist conditions.

OENOTHERA pumilis. It must have a position of full sun when, throughout summer it will bear its large yellow blooms on short, branching stems.

PENTSTEMON. Happy in full sun or partial shade, the rock pentstemons are delightful plants and to bloom in April and May one of the best is *P. Newberryi,* almost a shrub and which bears deep pink tubular flowers. *P. confertus* bears short spikes, creamy-yellow during May and June, whilst *P. pinifolius* has attractive pine-like foliage and bears its striking scarlet trumpets from June until September.

PHLOX subulata. With their dwarf habit and bearing sheets of richly-coloured blooms, this phlox is ideal for troughs, but should be planted near the sides. Very compact is the new Aunt May, which bears lavender-blue flowers; and plant near it Temiscaming, which covers itself in sheets of rich crimson.

POLYGONATUM Hookeri. A miniature Solomon's Seal, bearing in spring its dainty sprays of pale pink bells on only 3-in. stems.

POTENTILLA. Those useful for a trough or small rockery are of shrubby habit and remain in bloom throughout summer. Making a most attractive little plant 2 in. high is *P. verna pygmaea* having bottle-green foliage and bearing bright golden blooms. Lovely too, is *P. Tonguei,* which has silvery-green foliage and bears a bloom of rich apricot with a red centre.

PRIMULA. One or two of the Juliae hybrids, especially the very dwarf F. Ashby will be suitable for a trough, but amongst the most beautiful members of the family are the *P. pubescens hybrids.* Of auricula habit, the plants bear their bloom on stems from 3–5 in. in length and are in bloom from the end of March until mid-May. Extremely dwarf and free flowering is Gnome, which bears terra-cotta blooms with a striking golden centre. Striking too, with its rich crimson blooms is The Cardinal, whilst Mrs. J. H. Wilson bears a bloom of dark mauve with a creamy-white centre and is strongly fragrant. The plants are happiest in partial shade and in a compost containing some peat.

ROSE. The most compact of the miniature roses described in Chapter 2 are ideal plants for a trough.

SAXIFRAGE. The number of varieties are so large that a whole book could well be devoted entirely to them. They are amongst the most valuable plants for a trough garden, for almost all of them are of cushion habit though some bear their bloom in graceful sprays often 18–20 in. in length. For a trough, varieties of the Kabschia or Cushion section are most suitable. Excellent is *S. Jenkinsae* which forms a cushion of medium green over which cup-shaped blooms of clear pink are held on 1-in. stems. Equally lovely is Hindhead Seedling which bears primrose-yellow blooms over densely-tufted foliage, while Grace Farwell forms grey cushions over which salmon-red flowers are held.

SEDUM. Happiest in full sun, the stonecrops are excellent for sinks for late summer flowering. One of the best is *S. cauticolum* from Japan, with glaucous foliage and rosy flowers. Delightful too, is Coral Carpet, the pale green carpets turning a lovely coral-red; and *S. Douglassi*, whose foliage turns vivid scarlet and which bears yellow flowers on 6-in. stems.

SEMPERVIVUM. So easily propagated by offsets, the Houseleeks will thrive in the shallowest of soils and in a sun-baked position. There are more than a hundred species in cultivation and a large proportion are suitable for sink and trough gardens. Most attractive is *S. arachnoideum Stansfieldi*, the Cob-webbed Houseleek, the foliage turning a rich crimson. Interesting is *S. Borisii*, like a tiny woolly ball; and *S. Powelli*, the rosettes being green, pink and red.

SPIRAEA decumbens. This is a charming little plant for a shady trough and a peaty soil. It makes a little shrub 4 in. tall and through the latter weeks of summer bears its flat heads of purest white.

THALICTRUM Kiusianum. A native of Japan, this Maidenhair which grows only 3 in. tall has attractive fern-like foliage and bears tiny feathery-heads of deep lavender-rose.

VERONICA. With their shrub-like habit, the dwarf veronicas are amongst the most valuable plants for a trough garden. Most attractive is *V. cinerea* which has silver foliage and during early summer bears spikes of brilliant blue on 3-in. stems. Most colourful is *V. pectinata rosea* which forms a dense grey mat, its spikes of pale pink being held on 2-in. stems. A hybrid, Trehane has golden leaves and bears spikes of pale blue.

WAHLENBERGIA serpyllifolia. It likes a soil containing leaf mould and a sunny situation. It makes a compact plant of shrubby growth and during May bears huge bells of deep purple on 2-in. stems.

Miniature Trees and Shrubs for a Trough

ABIES balsamea. This is the Balsam Fir, which grows as broad as it does tall and rarely exceeds a height of 4–5 inches. The foliage is dark green, underlined silver.

ACER palmatum atropurpureum. This lovely miniature maple has beautifully cut foliage of rich purple-bronze, and is charming used as a specimen tree planted at one corner of the trough or sink.

ALYSSUM spinosum. A tiny shrublet growing to a height of 5–6 in. with pale silver-white foliage.

COTONEASTER. Like a miniature evergreen tree, which has glossy dark green foliage, the variety Stonefield Gnome, is a most suitable plant for a rockery or trough. It grows to a height of only 15 in. and at an early age looks extremely old.

CUPRESSUS. Several members of the large cupressus family are ideal for a trough garden and perhaps the best is *Cupressus obtusa juniperoides*, for at twenty years of age it will have reached a height of only 6 in. It has dark green foliage and a branched habit. Plant with it *C. nana aurea*, of similar habit and which has bright golden foliage.

GENISTA. For a sun-baked position, the miniature brooms are delightful plants bearing their tiny sweet pea-like flowers during the first weeks of summer. *G. januensis* grows only 6 in. tall and bears tiny yellow flowers, whilst *G. dalmantica* is like a dense miniature gorse only 4 in. tall and in May is covered in golden flowers.

HEDERA minima. This lovely little shrubby ivy will lift itself up a stone, twisting to a height of 7–8 in., and remaining evergreen all the year round. Plant *H. conglomerata* to trail along the sides of the trough.

HELICHRYSUM. The shrubby Everlasting Flowers are most attractive plants for a dry, sunny position and for a trough which may not receive much attention. *H. bellidoides* grows to a height of 4 in. and bears its white flowers early in summer; whilst *H. marginatum* bears dusky-pink flowers on tiny silver hummocks.

JASMINUM Parkeri. With their clear yellow bells, the jasmines are always appreciated and a delightful dwarf form is *J. Parkeri*, which makes a tiny shrub only 7–8 in. tall and is ideal for a trough or rockery. It bears its tiny yellow bells throughout mid-summer.

JUNIPER. Not all the Junipers are of familiar pencil-like habit and one of the most interesting is *J. Coxii*, like an evergreen weeping willow which grows only 5–6 in. high. Then there is the Carpet Juniper, *J. sabina tamariscifolia* with its feathery foliage and *J. communis compressa*, which forms an upright pencil-like plant of dense, feathery, glaucous green foliage. A horizontal form is called Bar Harbour, which has graceful soft green foliage.

SALIX Boydi. This tiny Willow is truly a remarkable tree reaching a height of 10 in. only after fifty years' growth. This little gem makes an ideal trough or miniature garden tree, its pale green dancing foliage being most attractive. Almost as dwarf is *S. Wehrahni*, a tiny pussy willow, covering itself with silver catkins throughout early spring.

SPRUCE. The dwarf spruces are amongst the most attractive

plants for a trough or small rockery. *Picea alba albertina*, a form of the White Spruce of Alberta, grows only one inch each year, whilst *P. excelsa Gregoryana* forms a tiny ball-like tree as if covered in needles. Also globular in form is *P. excelsa nana compacta*, the dwarf Norway Spruce which has horizontal branches.

Chapter 13

MAKING A MINIATURE ROCKERY

The value of a rockery – Suitable stone – Making a flat rockery – The raised rockery – Planting – Care of a rockery.

A ROCKERY will be an asset in many ways, however small the garden. It may be made as an alternative to a dry wall or bank where the garden may be of more than one level or where approached from a basement flat. A neat rockery garden made on either side of stone steps will provide an all-the-year-round interest. So often where the garden is approached from a lower level by means of steps, on either side of the steps is a grassy bank, useful for miniature bulbs but difficult to keep tidy except by constant clipping; or a low stone wall may have been constructed. This will be neat and of attractive appearance, but will generally be devoid of colour. A rockery, with the stones correctly laid to provide a natural appearance will be inexpensive to construct, whilst being easily maintained. It will also provide continuous colour, irrespective of adverse weather.

A small raised rockery may be made in a corner of a yard, at the point where two walls meet, or beneath a low wall where it may be observed from the house. The banking of the rockery would enable a larger number of plants to be grown than if made on the flat, whilst they could be revealed to greater advantage. Rockery stone may, however, be attractively used on the flat, possibly to surround a small pool or fountain at the centre of a small courtyard, or an almost flat rockery may be made along one side of a walled garden 3 ft. wide so that it will be possible to attend to it with ease; or it may be the focal point of a roof, or small garden which, except for the rockery, may possibly have been paved.

A miniature rockery need be no more than 4 ft. long and 3 ft. wide and may be made slightly raised above ground level to permit both the stone and the plants to reveal their full beauty whilst at the same time assisting drainage. A rockery need not be of large proportions to be a success, indeed a large rockery will demand considerable time in its maintenance, whilst where large sized stones are used, a rockery will often give the appearance of having been dumped from a lorry, there being little attempt to lay the stone to conform to natural lines. The stone of a well-made rockery should be quite inconspicuous, it should blend naturally with the surroundings and the lie of the land and where made on the flat, the stones should "fall" slightly in the same direction. As Reginald Farrer, that master of rockery, has said, "the rock garden must have a plan," in the same way that nature, too, has a purpose. The best effect is obtained if the flat side of the stone is placed uppermost, yet all too often the rockery, of whatever proportions it may be, has the appearance of Malayan pagodas, the stones being set with their points uppermost, though no stone has ever been weathered by nature in this way.

Suitable Stone

The most satisfactory stone in many ways to make a small rockery is Westmorland limestone, which is naturally formed in layers and which may be reproduced in a similar manner on the rockery. This stone is composed of billions of calceous forms of insect life in a highly compressed state and being porous permits the roots of the plants to penetrate, thus providing the cool, moist conditions, so essential to healthy plant life. This is additionally important where the rockery is in any way exposed to the sun and where there may be no great depth of soil. Again, this limestone is composed of cracks and crevices of various sizes which, when filled with compost, become miniature rock gardens in themselves and make the arranging of the plants a simple matter, the finished rockery having the appearance of great natural beauty.

Where making a small rockery, it is better to use stones of average size and as near as possible to a similar size throughout rather than to use dozens of small pieces, so often found with a rockery, and which will be difficult to arrange to present a natural appearance. Westmorland limestone may be obtained from the country, whilst rock garden constructors will generally have a supply in stock and will almost always have small quantities for disposal and deliver it. A quantity of fresh loamy soil, preferably sterilized, may also be obtainable from a local nurseryman and to this should be incorporated some grit to encourage drainage and a small quantity of moist peat to help the soil retain summer moisture. A quantity of boiler ash or similar material should be available for drainage at the base of the rockery and this may be collected and stored until ready to use.

Having obtained the stone, the making of the rockery should proceed slowly. It is generally believed that the more haphazard the stone is laid, the better will be the effect. This is far from being so, for much needs to be considered whilst the rockery is being constructed, if the effect, when finished, is to be as natural as possible.

Making a Flat Rockery

Where making a rockery on the flat, first remove the soil to a depth of approximately 4 in. and to the required measurements. A gentle slope which will be necessary for efficient drainage and to enable the plants to reveal their full beauty, should be made in a southerly direction wherever possible, though first consideration should be to construct it where it will be seen to best advantage from the house, or possibly from some other part of the garden. When this has been decided, the first stones should be set in position at one end. These will be the lower stones and should be placed with their flat surface uppermost. About 3 in. of stone should appear above the level of the surrounding ground. The remainder of the excavated area should be filled with clinker or ash to a depth of 2–3 inches and over this is placed 2–3 in. of soil. Another two or more stones are then pressed into the soil with their upper surface several inches above the stones first laid. They should be placed so that their surface is sloping in much the same direction as those first laid. In the space between the stones, the compost should be added, making it quite firm, especially about the stones, so that there will be no air pockets. Allow the soil to encroach over the lower stones so as to give a more natural effect. Additional stones should be laid in such a way as to prevent any formality and as the rockery is built up they should be placed on to a greater thickness of soil or the stones themselves may be of greater depth. Where making a rockery on the flat, it should gradually tail off so that the last stones to be laid will be about the same level as those first laid. The completed rockery will have the appearance of continuity as if weathered naturally rather than appear as if a volcanic eruption has taken place, where the stones have been thrown together without any attempt at following a natural rock formation. For the same reason, that glistening white spar stone, so often to be found pressed into mounds of soil with their points in pagoda fashion, should always be avoided.

The prepared compost should be added as the rockery is built up. This should be pressed around the stones and though it should be allowed to encroach over their surface, it should not be allowed to obscure the vertical front of the stones which is the most beautiful part of limestone rock. The compression of the compost about the stones is important to conserve moisture, in addition to eliminating air pockets. The soil should be of a reasonable depth, for if too shallow it will cause the roots of the plants to dry out during dry weather. The stone will, however, permit a large variety of plants to be grown due to its ability to maintain moisture below ground level. It is here, around the stones, that the rock plants like to have their roots, just as they do where growing naturally. If a stone be carefully lifted from an established rockery, the sides of the cavity left by the stone will be found to be a mass of threadlike roots, showing beyond doubt that the plants appreciate the cool, moist soil around the stones. Close to the stones ahould be planted those plants having a liking for moisture and where limestone is used, those which require lime in their diet. But no planting should be done until the completed rockery has been allowed time to consolidate when, after ten days or so it may be found necessary to "top up" with compost in those places where the soil has consolidated. Where planting on the flat, as great a depth of soil as possible should be provided and this is even more essential where the rockery is exposed to full sunshine.

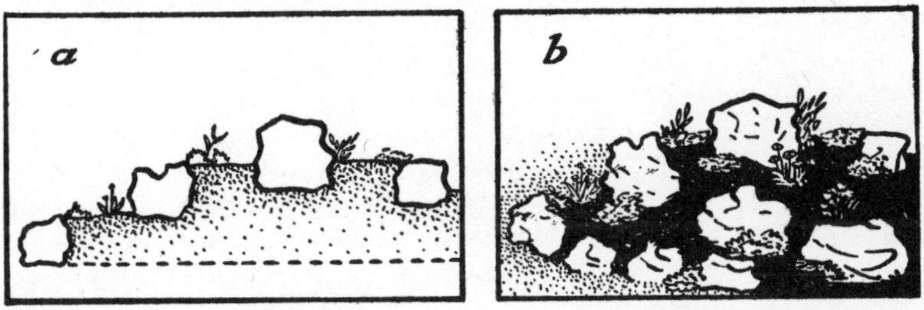

The Raised Rockery

To build a rockery on a low bank, the stone will be inserted into the bank after first removing the grass. Where possible, it should be the aim to give the completed rockery as natural an appearance as possible by following the suggestions already made, any haphazard laying of the stones with their unsightly points being eliminated. Here, stones should again be laid with their flat surface uppermost and each should slope gently in the same direction. It may not, however, be possible to build up the stones as gradually as desired and which always gives a rockery a more natural appearance, for this will be determined by the fall of the ground. It may be possible to extend the rockery by adding soil at the base, lessening the acuteness of the angle where the bank is unduly steep.

To lay the stone, it will be necessary to begin at the base by cut-

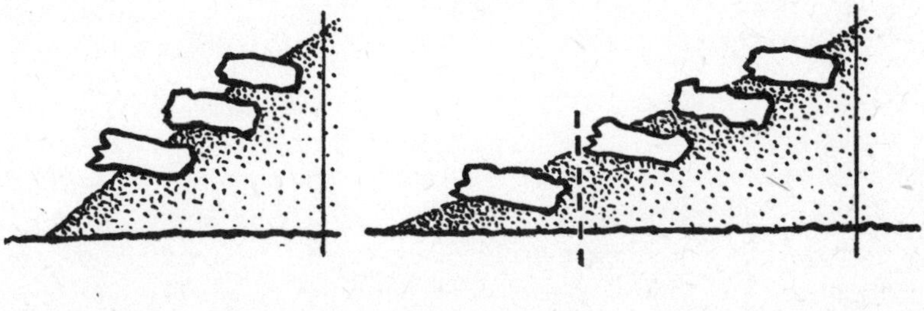

ting away soil to the dimensions of the stones and making certain that a sufficient portion of the stone will be beneath the soil when laid. The soil above the stones should be allowed to fall upon them, thus giving a more natural appearance. Make the stone quite firm and press soil firmly around the sides. Care should be taken to avoid a step-like appearance by planting in groups rather than placing one stone immediately above another.

Do not overdo the use of the stone, too much will produce a far worse effect than where using too little, but sufficient must be used to prevent the soil from falling down and obliterating the stones and plants.

Where making a rockery at the foot of a wall or in a corner, the rockery will be built up by degrees and it will first be necessary to provide a foundation. The core of the rockery may be of material which will have little value for use elsewhere and indeed most new gardens contain quantities of stone, broken bricks and mortar and all manner of unwanted material left behind by the builder. About an old property too, may generally be found broken pots and glass and other refuse which will need to be removed and which, with boiler ash and clinker, will be ideal for making a base for a rockery. Where no rubbish is available, a load of broken brick from a building site will be necessary. This will make for efficient drainage and help to raise the rockery. Over this fresh loam is placed, the stones being placed as previously described. Do not attempt to make the rockery too high or to use too much stone or pieces that are too large, for what could well be a most pleasing way of utilizing a colourless part of the garden, would become an uninteresting mass of stone rather than a rockery of beauty.

In making a rockery in this way, it will be essential to consolidate the soil as the rockery is built up, for if made over a heap of loose soil, the appearance will change as the mass consolidates, besides leaving harmful air pockets about the stones which may cause the plants to die back. As the stones are being laid, a mixture of loam, peat and grit should be pressed around and this should also be used for a top dressing. If the position is exposed to full sunshine, additional moist peat or leaf mould should be used, also where the acid-loving plants are to be used. It will be found that these are also shade lovers, so where growing in the often shaded situation of a town garden, it will be advisable to provide the shade-loving plants with the soil conditions they like.

Planting

Whilst almost all plants of compact habit will be suitable for a rockery, only the most dwarf plants should be used where the rockery is of miniature proportions. And whilst the new compact annuals will prove suitable, it is suggested that only the true alpines should be planted on a rockery. For here they will receive the natural conditions they could not obtain elsewhere in the garden. Being perennial, they will flourish over a long period, presenting the minimum of trouble with their upkeep. Those plants previously described for a trough or sink garden should be used, together with the most dwarf of the miniature bulbs. Plant the sun lovers and the shade lovers separately rather than mix them. A number of favourites will have to be omitted but one will have the satisfaction of knowing that given the conditions they require, the plants will be long lived and will bloom to perfection.

Planting should also be done with a view to having an all-year-round display rather than a liberal splash of colour only once or twice a year. This may be achieved by including small groups of the miniature winter and early spring flowering bulbs, double daisies and the Juliae primroses, also several of the hardy saxifrages, all of which bloom during the colder months. There will be no room for those plants of trailing habit, unless it be perhaps a single plant of the aubretia and trailing phlox to provide a sheet of colour which will be the focal point of the rockery, though any unduly long shoots must be kept cut back to keep the plants in bounds.

Plants for a town garden rockery must be able to withstand deposits of soot and sulphur, whilst those for an exposed position, such as a roof garden, must be completely hardy, which almost all alpine plants fortunately are. Though possibly the best time to make a rockery will be early in spring, especially where exposed and will thus enable the plants to become thoroughly established before winter, the plants from specialist growers are almost always grown in small pots and so may be planted at almost any time except when the soil is frozen. It will also be advisable to omit the generally dry months of May and June by planting in March or early April, in July, or early in autumn.

As only those plants of most compact habit will be grown, a more pleasing effect will be obtained if two are planted together, about 3 in. apart. Those of semi-trailing habit should be planted above a stone so that they may trail over the stones rather than use up valuable soil space required by other plants. The tiny bulbs may be planted in groups of three between other plants for they will have finished blooming before most other plants come into bloom. The moisture loving plants should be set close to the stones so that their roots can penetrate beneath the stones. They should also be planted about the lower parts of the rockery where moisture will tend to drain from above. Where possible, group together those plants which bloom at a similar time, those that bloom in spring, those that bloom in summer, with the autumn and winter flowering plants together so that there will be groups of rich colour rather than inconspicuous blooms dotted here and there about the rockery. Alpine plants love company and will always be happier in groups, though it must be remembered that most plants will make dense little bushes within a year or so and must be given room to develop.

Care of the Rockery

For the pot-grown plants, make a generous hole with a trowel so that their roots will be deeply planted and make them quite firm. Take care when removing the plants from the pots or papers in which they will have been despatched, to disturb the roots as little as possible, for most alpine plants resent disturbance. Water well when planting is completed and at all times see that the plants never lack moisture. This will mean watering during dry periods, but the plants will obtain great benefit from a peat mulch given in June. Moist peat, which should be pressed up to the crown of the plants, will provide the surface roots with moisture and a valuable rooting medium and thus maintain the health of the plants. A little well-decayed manure mixed with the peat will be appreciated by the plants after the rockery has been established for two years.

In autumn, the rockery should be weeded with care, pressing into the soil any alpine plants which have been disturbed and at the same time trimming any plants that have made excessive growth and are tending to choke their neighbours. A tangled mass of plant growth about a rockery will deprive each plant of its individual charm. It will also be advisable to lift a few plants every two or three years so that they may be divided, the old centre portion being discarded and the vigorous outer growth being replanted. There should soon be sufficient material to make another rockery or possibly to enlarge the existing one. Those plants which will not readily divide should be increased by cuttings, which are rooted in a gritty compost around the sides of a pot or pan. By careful trimming and propagation the life of the plants will be maintained indefinitely.

Work about the rockery, where bulbs have been planted, should proceed with care whether weeding or removing plants, so that the bulbs will not be disturbed, whilst where a rockery is given that extra attention to detail as to watering and mulching, the plants will respond with a display of great brilliance. The removal of weeds as soon as observed, the stirring of the soil between the plants following the winter snow and rains, syringing the plants with clean water in the cool of the evening during a period of hot, dry weather will be amply rewarded. A rockery well made and carefully tended will remain of constant interest.

PLANTS LIKING A CHALKY SOIL:

Achillea argentea
Aethionema
Androsace
Cyclamen
Dianthus
Helianthemum
Iris reticulata
Polygola
Ramondia
Saxifrage
Scabious alpina
Sedum
Soldanella alpina

PLANTS LIKING AN ACID SOIL:

Astilbe saxatilis
Calceolaria
Daboicia
Dicentra pusilla
Erica vulgaris
Gentiana sino-ornata
Lithospermum
Oxalis
Pennettya tasmanica
Primula
Thalictrum alpinum
Trillium undulatum
Vinca minor

PLANTS LIKING A SUNNY SITUATION:

Acantholimon
Achillea
Aethionema
Alyssum saxatile
Anchusa angustissima
Antennaria dioica
Arenaria
Calmisia
Cystisus
Dianthus
Doronicum
Genista
Helianthemum
Helichrysum
Iberis
Linaria
Pentstemon
Phlox
Potentilla
Raoulia
Sedum
Sisyrinchium
Thymus

PLANTS LIKING SHADE:

Ajuga
Andromeda pilifolia
Cassiope
Cyclamen
Epimedium
Erodium
Gaultheria
Gentiana
Hutchinsia
Lysimachia
Mentha requieni
Mimulus
Myosotis
Omphalodes
Polygonatum
Primula
Pulmonaria
Saxifrage (Mossy)
Spiraea
Tuberaria
Viola cornuta

Chapter 14

WINDOW BOX GARDENING

The use of a window box – Fixing the box – Making up the box – Filling the window box – Its care – Trailing plants – Hanging baskets.

WHERE there is no opportunity to enjoy gardening elsewhere, the window box presents a medium in which horticultural skill may be employed to the full, for it is surprising the wide variety of plants which, with a little ingenuity, may be made to reveal their full beauty from so small an area. There is a tendency to look upon the window box as being no more than a container to hold pots of geraniums or cinerarias, or for plants which can be given a sunny situation and constant attention. Nothing could be further from the case, for a well-prepared window box of smallest proportions may remain colourful throughout the year, whilst a wide variety of plants may be grown with the minimum of attention. Nor is it necessary for the box to be given a position of full sun, for many plants may be grown in semi-shade, including the lovely winter and spring flowering bulbs. Also in bloom during winter and spring are primroses and violas and these are followed by pansies and violettas for summer or the variegated or scented-leaf geraniums. These plants will, in fact, be happier away from the full heat of the sun. For a sunny situation the range is now enormous with the introduction of numerous miniature flowering annuals, the multiflora begonias and geraniums of compact habit whilst dozens of lovely bulbs may be grown, from the tiny chionodoxas to the more voluptuous double-flowering tulips. Indeed all those plants suggested elsewhere as being suitable for summer bedding may be used for a window box, depending upon its size, the smallest of the miniatures being suitable for a very small window. Nor is it necessary for a window box to be fixed only in front of a window. Boxes made to similar dimensions, so that there will be a reasonable depth of soil may be fixed to the wall of a courtyard. Where the walls are 6–7 ft. high a double row of boxes may be fixed, the lower boxes at a height of about 4 ft., with others 18 in. above. They should be fixed between the lower boxes so that when trailing plants are allowed to fall over the sides of the boxes they will in no way interfere with those boxes at a lower level.

It is essential that a window box should not be made too shallow, a depth of 6 in. being advisable with 5 in. as a minimum so that the roots of the plants will not dry out too quickly in summer and which would necessitate twice daily watering. The deeper the box the more labour saving it will be and where a number of boxes are being used, watering is an important factor. Anything that will reduce watering to a minimum must be done, the careful preparation of the soil and the making up of the box contributing to this in no small way. To some extent the size of box will be dictated by the size of the window, for the box must be to scale or it will harm the appearance of the property. The large windows of a Georgian house will permit the window box to be made 8 in. deep, whereas the long, low mullioned window of a cottage will mean that the box must be made no more than 6 in. deep. The length too, will be determined by the length of the window. Where boxes are being fixed to the

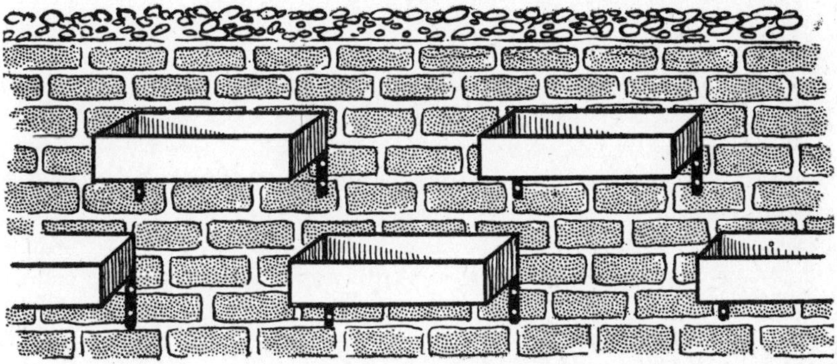

wall of a courtyard or merely placed on blocks around a paved terrace, a veranda or yard, they may of course be made to any reasonable size depending upon where they are to be placed. Long, narrow boxes could be used around the sides of a yard or terrace in place of tubs, where space is strictly limited.

Fixing the Box

The correct fixing of the window box is all-important and here again this will be governed by the structure. A window with a wooden frame will present few difficulties provided the box is made to the exact dimensions of the frame. Here, a strong iron bracket may be fixed to the top of the sides of the box and to the frame of the window, and in this way the box should be quite secure. This is most important for it must be remembered that a window box filled with soil must carry a considerable weight especially when the soil is wet. There must also be no danger to those walking below, either through the box falling or through falling soil. It must be remembered that where fixing the box, it must permit the opening of the window as well as the watering and planting of the box without undue difficulty. Owing to the considerable weight of a box when filled, it should be fixed into position when empty, boxes which are easily reached being filled from outside, those fixed to an upper room window being filled from inside.

Where a box has to be fixed to a stone or brick wall, into which the brackets are to be fastened, the wall must first be plugged to a depth of not less than 2 in. into which the screws are fixed. To give added efficiency in making the box secure, strong galvanized wires should be fastened from the outer edge of the box sides to a position on the wall above the bracket. This will take some of the strain of a box in which may be growing winter and spring flowering plants and which may have become unduly heavy by continuous rains or a fall of snow.

Being less heavy, a wooden box is preferable to one of concrete, whilst it is more easily constructed and fixed. A wooden box made of 1-in. timber, treated on the inside with preservative and painted on the outside will prove extremely long lasting. One suggestion is that two boxes are used to maintain the display, one to be placed inside the other. For example, whilst the original box will continue with the summer display of annuals or geraniums right through autumn, these plants may be replaced by an inner box made up of bulbs and other winter flowering plants which will come into bloom as soon as placed in the permanent box, possibly in November. Or again, whilst the fixed box may be planted with plants and bulbs to bloom from Christmas until March, the second box will be planted to provide colour from April until early June. Yet another method is to allow the original spring display to continue until the end of May and then to replace with an inner box made up of annuals sown directly in the box in early April, possibly in a frame. There will thus be few periods when the window box will not be showing colour. The inner box, made of wood, may be fitted inside a fixed box constructed either of wood or of concrete. It is placed in by "handles" of cord at either end and which are removed when the box is in position. A second box may be used in much the same way as where plants are grown in pots and brought on either in the home or in the greenhouse to maintain a succession of bloom. It is preferable that the inner or replacement box be of wood rather than of metal, for plants are never happy when their roots are in a non-porous container, however well drained it may be. For the same reason, a window box should be constructed either of concrete or of wood. These are porous materials and also possess a rough inner surface which is conducive to vigorous root action.

Making the Box

As a window box has to carry a considerable weight of soil, it should be constructed of 1 in. wood, cut to the correct lengths and planed. The front and back of the box should be cut to the length required, the ends fitting inside. When cutting the ends, allow for the thickness of wood so as to keep to the correct overall measurements required. If any attempt is made to dovetail the corners it should be remembered that the strength of a dovetail lies in the perfection of its construction and a water-resistant glue should be used. Always bear in mind that a good, simple job is better than a bad complicated one. When securing the two ends no advantage will be gained by using screws instead of 2 inch nails, for when driven in they only tend to part the grain, thus splitting the wood. For additional strength at the corners an angle bracket should be screwed either on the inside or outside of the box.

Adequate drainage holes should be made in the base, preferably making a dozen or so holes of ½-in. diameter rather than half the number of 1 in. diameter, to ensure that there will be little of the compost escaping. Where possible always use hard wood, such as seasoned oak, in the construction of the box, or failing that, American Red Cedar, both of which will remain almost impervious to moisture through the years and neither of which require painting as a preservative.

After the box has been made up it should be treated on the inside with a wood preservative, Cuprinol being most efficient. This treatment is especially necessary if the box has been constructed of deal or other soft wood. Thoroughly soak the inside of the box and allow it to remain in the open after treating for at least ten days until it has become thoroughly weathered and any fumes which might be injurious to plant life will have escaped. The box may then be painted on the outside only, to conform to one's tastes, or to the colour scheme of the house. The window box should be of the same colour as the window frames; turquoise, grey, or pale blue being most attractive, also cream or white. These shades seem to bring out the rich colours of the blooms to the utmost advantage. Against stone or mullioned windows then a box made of oak presents a better appearance if it is not painted. Filled with crimson geraniums the effect is extremely rich. Where the boxes are to be used against the white or cream washed walls of a cottage, a pleasing effect will be to paint the boxes and window frames pale blue or pink. Always use one of the more delicate colours, deep greens and brown never looking right for window boxes.

Owing to the weight of soil the boxes are always fixed before they are filled, though it is preferable to add the drainage materials first. And always remember to place the boxes where they can be easily attended. To place them in some inaccessible position which necessitates the use of a pair of steps to give them attention, or where the watering-can has to be held at arm's length above one's head, will be to make window box gardening a toil rather than a pleasure.

It should be said that a box which is to be used inside the fixed box should be constructed of ¾-in. wood to make its manipulation as easy as possible. An inner box, in which plants are already coming into bloom must, of course, be moved with the compost already in, and for this reason will be more easily used for those windows which may easily be reached from outside.

Filling the Box

Before placing any compost in the boxes it will be necessary to ensure thorough drainage. First the drainage holes in the base must be made so that the soil does not fall through, and this is best done by placing a piece of fine mesh wire netting over the base. Then add a layer of crocks to a depth of about ½ in. to ensure efficient drainage during winter. Over the crocks, a layer of turves placed grass downwards will occupy another 1½ in. of the box. The remaining space, depending upon the depth of the box, is filled with prepared compost.

The soil should preferably be taken from pasture, or be a good quality loam from a country garden, and where the soil is not troubled by deposits of soot and sulphur. Soil taken from a town garden will generally be of an acid nature and will also contain a large number of weed seeds. Therefore pasture loam is greatly to be preferred. A satisfactory compost will be made up by mixing:

3 parts loam
1 part peat
1 part grit or coarse sand (by weight).

Allow 2 lb. of ground limestone or lime rubble to a box 3 ft. long and 6 in. deep; 4 oz. of bone meal, a slow-acting fertilizer and a sprinkling of superphosphate which encourages a vigorous root action.

Whilst the same compost will not suit all plants a compromise may be made. For instance, geraniums prefer decayed manure to peat, whilst with begonias the reverse is the case. Most annuals, bulbs, and spring flowering plants will be happy where either peat or decayed manure is used, or half and half of each, which mixture would also prove acceptable both to begonias and geraniums.

It is important to make up a well-drained, friable compost, yet it must also be able to retain moisture during dry periods in summer. For this reason the peat or decayed manure, or a little of both, should not be omitted, and where the loam is of a light, sandy nature, then a larger proportion of humus materials should be added. It is important to keep the compost sweet as long as possible without the continual changing of the soil. Therefore lime in some form should not be omitted. A few pieces of charcoal in the soil will also help to maintain sweetness. Correctly prepared, the compost will not only make for healthy and vigorous plant growth, but will require changing only once every three years.

The window boxes, after they have been made quite secure, should be filled several days before they are to be planted so that the compost is allowed time to settle down. The compost is best taken to the boxes in a small bucket, and as it is placed in the box it should be pressed around the sides so that all air pockets will be eliminated. The box should be filled to the top and be allowed three or four days in which to settle down before any planting is done. The compost will then sink to about $\frac{1}{2}$ an inch below the top of the box which will allow for watering without the soil splashing over the side.

Care of the Box

Where only one box is being used planting will take place towards the end of May for the summer flowering plants and these will be replaced towards the end of October, with those plants which are to bloom during winter and spring. Much will, however, depend upon the plants to be used. For example, if winter flowering pansies are being grown with dwarf primroses, all that will be necessary to prolong the display through summer will be to remove carefully the primroses in May after flowering and to replace with summer flowering pansies or violas, the winter flowering varieties continuing to bloom until that time. Nothing could be more labour saving nor give a display of richer colour over so long a period and for so little outlay. The primroses could be grown on under a shady tree or in boxes in shade, to be transferred to the window box again in autumn. It will then be better to destroy the pansies and make a fresh planting.

Or maybe a display of geraniums will be required for the summer, in which case the plants may be grown on in pots in a greenhouse or warm room so that they will be showing colour when planted in the boxes in May to replace the spring plants. There will thus be no period of the year when the boxes are not colourful, which would also be the case where annuals are used. This delay may be overcome by using an inner box, which will enable the annuals to be planted early in April. If half-hardy plants, they will be grown on until mid-May in a small greenhouse or beneath a frame light, if hardy, they may be grown on in the box in the open. By planting early they will have made considerable growth by the time they are moved to the permanent box in early summer and will come quickly into bloom.

When the plants are changed in autumn, the soil should be given a dusting with hydrated lime to maintain sweetness whilst in spring, 2 oz. of bone meal should be worked into the compost. After three years, the soil should be replaced, the old compost being removed with a trowel and placed in a bucket after which the window box may be removed, cleaned, sterilized and replanted before fresh soil and drainage materials are replaced.

The boxes will require very little attention apart from watering and the occasional removal of dead blooms to prevent seeding so as to prolong the display. It should be remembered that the window box will often be protected by the eaves of a house and will thus receive little natural moisture. Where this is so, additional moisture must be provided from early April until mid-September though where the box is more exposed, watering should be necessary only during dry periods. Where facing due south, a window box will require more attention in this respect than where it does not receive the direct rays of the sun. It may be found that the compost of a box in a northerly position or where facing due east, will not dry out even during the heat of summer and will require watering only once each week. Violas and pansies especially will flourish under such conditions.

It will be advisable to use those plants most suited to certain conditions. Geraniums and a number of annuals will thrive in full sun and in a dry soil and should always be grown where it is not possible to give the window box regular waterings. Begonias on the other hand, though enjoying a sunny position, must have plenty of moisture about their roots if they are to remain long in bloom. There are also those plants which are happier growing under cool conditions, away from the rays of the mid-day sun.

All plants will appreciate a syringing with cold water during the cool of a summer evening and this will prevent them "flagging" and guard against red spider during dry weather. When watering, give the box a thorough soaking so that the moisture reaches the lower roots, but do not give so great an amount that it will percolate through the bottom of the box and cause annoyance to those who pass beneath. Where the box is to be left unattended for longer than usual, the soil should first be given a thorough soaking and small flat stones should then be pressed in between the plants. This will prevent too rapid evaporation during a hot period. During August, most plants will benefit from an occasional watering with liquid manure, obtainable from most seedsmen in concentrated form of a proprietary brand. A small watering can with a long spout will make for easier watering of window boxes and hanging baskets and no more than a gallon of water should be handled at one time or the simple task of watering will prove onerous. Watering is best done during early evening when the sun is off the boxes.

Trailing Plants

All those plants of compact habit previously described will be suitable for window box culture, taking care to select those plants which are happiest under certain conditions. There are also a number with a trailing habit which are most attractive for covering the sides of a window box, vase or tub, or for trailing from a hanging basket. They cannot be classed as miniature plants but are indispensable for this type of gardening. Most of them are extremely beautiful plants.

GERANIUM. All the trailing ivy-leaf varieties are suitable for a window box and amongst the best are Mrs. W. Clifton, with its double blood-red blooms; Sir Percy Blakeney, crimson; and Beauty of Castlehill, rose-pink. Each bears a fully double bloom. Excellent too, is L'Elegante, which has bottle-green leaves, edged with cream and is lovely for planting with those ivy-leaf varieties bearing richly coloured flowers.

LOBELIA. The only trailing variety is called Sapphire, its blooms borne in cascade fashion being of a deep sapphire-blue colour with a conspicuous white eye. It may be propagated from cuttings taken in early October and inserted in sandy soil, or it may be raised from seed sown in gentle heat in January. Most nurserymen will, however, have plants for sale in May for planting to the front of the window box and around the side of a vase, tub or hanging basket.

NASTURTIUM. The best variety for hanging baskets is a fully double salmon-red, propagated only by rooting the cuttings in sandy soil in September. For best results transplant into 2½-in. pots in November. The plants have a trailing habit and bloom profusely, and should be planted round the sides of a basket.

The double Gleam Hybrids are also very beautiful and if allowed to grow away without any stopping, make an excellent display with their vivid scarlet, salmon, gold and yellow blooms which are larger but perhaps not so dainty in formation as the double salmon-red form described above.

NEPETA. It is not the common form of nepeta or catmint used for edging a border that is used for its trailing habit, but the trailing, variegated leaf form. The best way of increasing stock is to plant several plants in a bed of soil where during summer they will send out their long strawberry-like runners and will take root at the leaf joints in a similar way. The individual plants may then be lifted and potted and grown on in a cold frame for using in baskets, vases or tubs. Being quite hardy, planting may take place at any time, the small cream and green leaves giving an appearance of considerable lightness.

PETUNIA. Though not of true trailing habit, the older, long-jointed varieties with their lightness of habit are valuable plants for a basket, vase or tub. Plants are raised from seed sown in heat in the New Year or they may be purchased from a nurseryman for planting out in May. Amongst the best varieties are General Dodds, crimson; Blue Bee, violet; and Rose King, with its attractive white throat.

PHLOX Drummondii. Whilst the *nana compacta* varieties are now used entirely for bedding and for window box culture, the older *grandiflora* varieties make excellent vase and basket plants with their loose, semi-trailing habit. They make up a charming vase display, planted with Sapphire lobelia and the ivy-leaf geraniums. Use a pink geranium with Cinnebar-scarlet phlox, or use crimson and white geraniums with rose-pink phlox, Brilliant, and allow Sapphire lobelia to trail over the sides.

TRADESCANTIA. The trailing variegated-leaf *Tradescantia fluminensis*, so often seen growing as an indoor pot plant, may successfully be used for hanging baskets and window boxes during summer. Like L'Elegante geranium, the plants should be taken indoors in October when they will continue to remain colourful throughout the winter. The silver leaves are striped with green and mauve, making a most colourful display when planted with scarlet ivy-leaf geraniums, especially the vivid scarlet double flowered Mrs. W. A. R. Clifton. Propagation is from cuttings taken at almost any time of the year. They will root readily in a sandy compost round the side of a pot in a room window. The geraniums may also be rooted in a similar way and so both plants may be used together where neither garden nor greenhouse is available.

Hanging Baskets

Suspended from the high wall of a courtyard, or from the eaves of a bungalow, where the baskets may be tended without difficulty, or suspended around a yard or tiny garden from stout wire supported by angle iron stakes, a hanging basket will provide a display of lightness and rich colour which will be difficult to equal in any other form of gardening. Where there is no garden, only a yard or surroundings quite devoid of colour, hanging baskets should be used as numerously as possible for they will bring beauty to the most drab surroundings.

The wire baskets may be obtained from most large nurserymen and sundriesmen for a few shillings, and carefully made up and maintained will remain colourful from June until the end of October. Requiring watering almost daily during dry periods, they should be hung where they may easily be reached and also where water, dripping from the baskets, will cause no inconvenience to others.

The baskets are made of a strong galvanized wire fastened closely together which ensures that the compost does not fall through, yet at the same time permits excess moisture to drain away. In making up the baskets they should first be lined to a depth of 1 in. with new sphagnum moss which will not only restrain the compost from falling through the wires but will help to absorb the moisture. Then place round the base a piece of new turf, with the soil side to the centre, and carefully mould it to the exact shape of the basket. Then to within 2 in. of the top of the basket is placed the prepared compost. This should consist of turf loam to which is added some decayed manure, a sprinkling of lime to keep it sweet, and a little bone meal to provide a constant source of plant food right through the summer.

Perhaps the best method of making up the basket is to set the plants as the basket is being filled with soil. In this way, they may be placed between the moss and wires with their roots in the soil. Three or four plants should be set around the basket immediately above the turf base. The roots should then be covered with 2–3 in. of compost when additional plants will be inserted. These will be those plants of trailing habit, *Phlox Drummondii*, petunias and nasturtiums. At the top of the basket will be planted either large flowered or pendant begonias to ivy or variegated leaf geraniums together with other plants noted for their lightness of habit such as the ageratum, nemesia, petunia and marguerite.

From early May the baskets may be made up and placed outdoors and should there be any risk of frost during that month, a piece of muslin may be placed over the baskets at nightfall. From the beginning, the plants must never be allowed to lack moisture and regular attention in this respect should continue until the baskets have finished flowering, when they should be emptied and stored until ready to be used again the following summer.

Chapter 15

VEGETABLES FOR THE SMALL GARDEN

Where vegetables may be grown – Beans, Broad – Beans, French – Beetroot – Broccoli – Brussels Sprouts – Cabbage – Carrot – Cauliflower – Celeriac – Hamburg Parsley – Kale – Lettuce – Marrow – Mushrooms – Onion – Pea – Radish – Savoy – Tomato.

By growing the most compact new varieties, it is possible to enjoy fresh vegetables from the smallest of gardens, but all vegetables appreciate sunshine and where the garden is shaded, which most walled gardens and those of congested town properties usually are, it will be better to concentrate on flowering plants. Fresh vegetables, however, are always appreciated, especially the summer salads which cannot be obtained in the pre-packed and frozen form and where space permits, they should be grown. Also, whereas tomatoes may be grown in tubs or deep boxes with success, most vegetables require the open ground and a soil well enriched with humus especially in the form of annual manures. Where space permits then, a small part of the garden, especially the small country garden where situated a distance from shops, could with advantage be set aside for vegetables of compact habit. A low hedge or a length of lattice fencing about 4 ft. high may be used to hide the generally unsightly vegetables, though care must be taken not to deprive the plants of valuable sunlight.

The ground at one's disposal need not cover an area of more than 6 ft. × 5 ft. and before any planting is done it should be cleaned of all perennial weeds and thoroughly enriched, for vegetables will not grow in an impoverished soil. Where well-decayed animal manures are difficult to obtain, old mushroom bed compost, used brewer's hops or hop manure of a proprietary brand, wool shoddy or seaweed, for coastal gardens, will prove equally suitable, for they will provide the necessary plant food in addition to the moisture holding humus which is so essential to healthy growth. Where grown in a humus-laden soil, vegetables will have a rich, succulent quality, crisp and full of flavour, and will taste very differently from those to be obtained from a shop, which may have travelled a considerable distance in warm weather, and will almost certainly have been grown with the aid of artificial fertilizers.

Where space is strictly limited, it will be necessary to grow only those vegetables which may be classed as being 'choice' and which are of greatly improved flavour when used directly from the garden. Cabbages and potatoes, turnips and celery, which occupy considerable space are best left to the commercial grower with a large area of land and mechanical methods of cultivation at his disposal. Tomatoes should be grown in boxes or tubs, as previously described, against the sunny wall of a yard or garden, but for the vegetable 'plot', dwarf beans, lettuce, radishes, dwarf cauliflowers, beetroot and several more crops may be grown to provide fresh vegetables almost the whole year round. A row of barn-type cloches will also increase the seasons and make it possible to enjoy winter lettuce and an early crop of French beans in addition to their being useful in other ways about the garden.

BEANS, Broad. Most broad beans grow rather too tall for a tiny garden, but The Sutton, which recently received an Award of Merit grows only 12 in. high and requires no staking. Extremely hardy, the beans may be sown in autumn for an early crop, sowing 6–8 in. apart and 2 in. deep. The plants are of branched, bushy habit, unlike most broad beans, whilst they bear a heavy crop.

BEANS, French. This is one of the most useful of all vegetables for growing in a tiny garden, for a dozen or so plants, occupying a row 6 ft. in length will provide delicious beans from the end of June, where grown under cloches until early autumn where grown unprotected. Two rows should therefore be planted and for an early crop, sow about twenty-four seeds of Sutton's Premier under cloches planting them 3 in. apart. Thin out to 6 in. when it may be seen exactly how many have germinated. Sow early in April and where all may have germinated transplant alternate beans, making a row alongside the cloches. This should be done towards the end of May when danger of frost should have departed, for French beans are somewhat tender. Those under cloches will mature at the end of June, those in the open being ready for gathering a month later. To ensure that there will be sufficient plants for both purposes, it will be advisable to plant an additional dozen or so seeds under a cloche at one end of the row. Plant the seed 1–2 in. deep and keep the soil moist and friable as beans do not grow well under dry conditions. Seed may, of course, be sown in the open ground about May 1st or in boxes in a small frame, the plants being set out at the month's end.

As the dwarf bean is one of the heaviest cropping of all vegetables considering the amount of ground the plants occupy and is also one of the most appreciated, readers may like to know of other interesting and delicious varieties. Excellent is Brown Beauty, so called because of the colour of its seed for the beans are pale yellow, of splendid flavour whilst it crops heavily. Delicious too, is the Green Snap Bean, which bears a profusion of tiny curved, deep green beans which are quite stringless and should be cooked whole. To crop well into autumn from an early June sowing is the romantically named, Keeney's Stringless Refugee, an enormous cropper of succulent beans.

BEETROOT. For pickling, a row of beetroot sown along one side of a small plot will provide sufficient to fill several jars. It will be at its best, sweet and juicy, pulled when about the size of a tennis ball, those large round roots so often being woody and bitter. Detroit Globe is an excellent variety, free from any 'rings' when cooked, whilst the new Non-Bleeding, with which it is not necessary to screw off the tops and treat with care as with the others, is also good.

The seed is sown early in May, the plants being thinned to 3 in. apart. As it is a maritime plant, it will appreciate 1 oz. per yard of common salt mixed with the soil before drilling. The plants should be kept watered during a dry period.

BROCCOLI. The most compact of the hardy broccoli is Dobbie's Royal Oak, of dwarf, compact habit. It is so valuable in that if necessary it will stand through the severest of winters and be at its best early the following summer, a time when there are few vegetables in the shops. The white heads are not large, but are most solid and possess a rich flavour. The seed should be sown in May when the heads will be ready for cutting in exactly twelve months.

BRUSSELS SPROUTS. They require plenty of manure, a long season to mature and firm planting if stems of tightly packed sprouts are to be obtained to use through winter. The two most suitable varieties for a small garden are The Wroxton and The Darlington, the former being later to mature. Both are of very compact habit, growing to only half the height of that of the new Cambridge introductions which are more suited to field culture. The sprouts are fairly small with no loose leaves about them and they eat like juicy nuts. Seed should be sown at the end of March for they like a long season and as soon as large enough to handle, the young plants should be set 12 in. apart, planting firmly into consolidated soil.

CABBAGE. The large drumhead varieties cannot be recommended for the small garden. Two, however, are excellent, and their names are Primo and Golden Acre. Both make small ball-like plants and have a delicate flavour and tenderness unknown in any other variety. From a spring planting, seed having been sown early in March, they will be ready for cutting towards the end of summer and will vacate the ground in time for winter lettuce to be planted under cloches. Plant 8 in. apart and plant firmly to encourage them to form solid hearts.

CARROT. A row or two of carrots may be sown along one side of a small plot where their feathery foliage will be most pleasing. This, however, is a crop better suited to commercial culture and should be grown in the small garden only to use when young and sweet, as a delicacy rather than for the stock-pot in winter.

Like all roots it should be grown quickly, otherwise the roots become hard and stringy and completely lack flavour. To have delicious young roots means that the seed must be sown in a soil rich in humus so that moisure is retained during dry periods. Sow thinly in early April and thin to 1 in. apart, it not being necessary to thin more fully owing to the plants being pulled long before they have matured. They should be used when the roots are about 3 in. long, and the best variety for this purpose is the new Morse's Bunching, which has a long stump root quite free of hard core.

CAULIFLOWER. Like the cabbage, only the most compact will be suitable for a small garden and Dean's Early Snowball is the best. It matures quickly and early and forms small, but very compact heads of purest white which possess a delicate flavour. Seed should be sown early in spring in a small seed bed enriched with some peat and the seedlings transplanted as soon as large enough to handle, planting them 12 in. apart and planting lettuce between.

CELERIAC. This is a root with the exact flavour of celery and for the small garden it is a valuable vegetable for it occupies so little space. Combined with its celery flavour is a distinct nuttiness and baked and served with beef and horseradish sauce it has few equals as a winter vegetable. Seed is best sown under cloches towards the end of March for it takes rather longer than most in germinating. Thin to 4 inches apart and never allow the plants to lack moisture. Sowing and planting is done on the flat, unlike celery there is no blanching and no earthing-up. Where transplanting, allow the bulbous-like roots to sit just on top of the soil and water continuously until the plants are established.

Towards the end of September soil should be scraped away from the top of the roots and any unwanted shoots removed from the roots with a sharp knife. Early in November the roots should be lifted, trimmed and the tops cut off. They should be stored in a box of sand or peat and used when required. The roots, which should be peeled before cooking may be used in several ways. They may be grated for winter salads or for cheese sandwiches; they may be cut into slices and fried, or boiled for serving with meat. Giant Prague is the best variety.

HAMBURG PARSLEY. This is a parsnip-like root having the

flavour of parsley and like the celeriac may be used in numerous ways, fried or boiled. It is better for the small garden than the parsnip for it does not make such a large root, whilst it is easier to grow. The tops also possess the flavour of parsley and as the roots occupy the ground through winter, being lifted only when required, the leaves may be used for flavouring. It likes a long season so the seed should be sown in March, the young plants being thinned to 8 in. apart.

KALE. Curled kale is a delicious green food for mid-winter, steamed in a little butter or margarine. Most types are much too tall and bushy for a small garden, but two or three plants of the hardy Dwarf Green will provide occasional and much-appreciated pickings throughout the winter. It makes a compact, bushy plant and should be planted 15 in. apart.

LETTUCE. For a small garden the magnificent Webb's Wonderful, like a huge crisp cabbage, is out of the question. Instead, for summer eating sow Tennis Ball, a delicately flavoured pale green cabbage lettuce which forms a small compact heart. It may be planted only 6 in. apart. Those who prefer a cos lettuce should grow Prince of Wales, for it is of compact, upright habit, is less liable to "bolt" during dry weather than others and it is self-folding, there being no need for any laborious tying to obtain a blanched heart.

For planting in early autumn under cloches, indeed it may also be grown without protection for cutting through summer and autumn, the little cabbage lettuce, Tom Thumb, is ideal and hardy enough to withstand a severe winter under cloches, or an average winter in the south unprotected.

For lettuce, the soil should not be of an acid nature, which most town garden soils generally are, for such a condition will cause the lettuce to be limp and slimy rather than that crisp freshness which is the hall-mark of a good lettuce. Indeed, few vegetables will be happy in an acid soil, so give a liberal dressing with hydrated lime each year in autumn.

MARROW. In a sunny corner, those who have epicurean tastes, should grow one or two plants of that wonderful South American marrow, the Avocadella. Cooked and served cold with oil or salad cream, its orange-coloured flesh is more delicious than any vegetable. It makes a plant of bushy habit, the fruits like oranges in size but green in colour, are borne at the centre during September and October.

Seed may be raised in small pots in the window of a warm room, or it may be sown outdoors directly into a small mound of hot manure and soil, over which is placed a closed cloche. The seed should be sown towards the end of April with their pointed end uppermost. The young plants should be kept covered with a cloche, or with a large jam jar, until early June though fresh air may be given during the day when cold winds are not troublesome. Never at any time allow the plant to become dry or the fruit will fail to swell. The avocadella is not a large marrow, the fruit being removed as soon as it attains the size of a large orange for then it will be at its best.

ONION. Whilst the ordinary onion and the leek are rather too robust for the very small garden, the spring onion and the chive, so useful for flavouring, may be grown. The chive, like the Japanese Bunch-onion, makes a compact tuft composed of dozens of grass-like leaves. These are cut off at ground level, cut into small pieces and used in salads, and for flavouring in many other ways. Fresh leaves will continue to form, whilst the plants may be increased by root division in autumn. Half a dozen plants will provide flavouring over a long period.

Spring onions too, are indispensable for summer salads. By making a sowing in autumn it will be possible to pull the onions in spring when they are most appreciated, whereas from a spring sowing, they would not be large enough to pull until well into summer. Sow the seed in drills in a rich soil and do no thinning.

PEA. Whilst most varieties, with their tall, bushy habit and need for staking are unsuitable for a small garden, occupying more space than their cropping powers warrant, also by their height depriving nearby plants of sunlight, there are several which are extremely dwarf. For those who appreciate something different in their diet, the Asparagus Pea, not of the same order as the garden pea, is an excellent plant for a small garden. It grows less than 12 in. tall, but makes a spreading plant. Give the same treatment as for dwarf beans for it is not quite hardy. Sow two seeds together 9–10 in. apart, removing one seedling when it is seen that both have germinated. The small pods, which should be steamed in their entirety and eaten with brown bread and butter, possess the true asparagus flavour.

Of the garden peas, it is those that crop early which are of dwarf habit. Of the main crop varieties, Onward, the best of all peas, grows a little over 2 ft. in height and though the most compact in this group, it is rather too tall for a very small garden. Two of the best early cropping peas, both of which grow only 16–18 in. tall and require only a few tigs to keep them above the ground, are Kelvedon Wonder, the earliest to mature and which has long, dark green pointed pods, and Little Marvel, the pods being borne in pairs. Both crop heavily. A double row should be sown in a wide drill, spacing the peas 1 in. apart each way.

RADISH. Even the smallest gardens can generally find room for a row or two of radishes to eat with the lettuce. To have them crisp and succulent and free of that hot bitterness which makes for unpleasant eating, a radish needs to be grown quickly in a rich soil well supplied with moisture holding humus and it needs to be eaten fresh from the garden. To grow under cloches, sow Saxa, a new brilliant scarlet variety of rapid maturity and for outdoor sowing, French Breakfast which is crimson tipped white at the base. The seed should be sown in a humus-laden soil, peat being excellent for this, and sow either broadcast or in shallow drills and keep well watered during dry weather.

For winter eating, the China Rose radish should be sown. It forms a large crimson root of blunt, tubular form and should be stored in moist sand during winter, to use when required. Seed should be sown in drills in early July, the seedlings being thinned to 3 in. apart and they are lifted towards the end of October.

SAVOY. For winter use, this is a valuable vegetable, but one only, Tom Thumb, is suitable for a small garden. A savoy is never at its best until it has been subjected to hard frost and so should not be used until after Christmas. A dozen plants will provide valuable mid-winter green together with Brussels Sprouts. From an early May sowing, Tom Thumb, will have formed small, compact heads by the year end, its dark green crinkled leaves having a pleasantly mild flavour. Where space permits, a slightly larger growing variety, Early Dwarf Ulm, which matures early, may also be grown.

TOMATOES. Requiring no staking and possessing the ability to ripen their fruit more quickly than the orthodox varieties, the new dwarf tomatoes, The Amateur and Pixie are of compact, bushy habit, and bear heavily. Neither do the plants require stopping. They are in fact almost foolproof and are very suitable for tub culture, three plants being planted to the average size tub. The plants may be raised in heat, sowing the seed in a greenhouse in February, or plants may be obtained from a nursery. Whichever method is used they should not be planted out before June 7th, when the plants should be showing the first truss of bloom. Some manure in the soil will increase the weight of the crop, also weekly applications of dilute manure water. As the fruit commences to ripen, clean wood wool or straw should be placed round the plants to prevent soil splashing on the fruit and causing loss through decay. The first fruit will be ripe before the end of July and the plants should continue to crop until the end of September when the tubs may be planted with winter and spring flowering plants.

Chapter 16

FRUIT FOR A SMALL GARDEN

Apples – Gooseberries – Hybrid Berries – Pears – Plums – Strawberries.

THOUGH there will be little opportunity for planting a bush or standard fruit tree in a garden of handkerchief size, except perhaps a single tree for its ornamental value when, because of pollination difficulties, it could not be expected to bear much fruit, it will be possible to enjoy fresh fruit by planting cordons or horizontal trained trees against a wall. Whilst pears and plums may be grown against a sunny wall, apples should be confined to the open, though they are most successful when grown in tubs about a courtyard. Gooseberries are another fruit which bear heavily in the cordon form and enjoying partial shade, they are, like the strawberry, quite happy in a town garden. Both the gooseberry and strawberry will bear heavily where few other crops could otherwise be grown. And is there anything more delicious than a matured dessert gooseberry eaten straight from the tree on a warm July morning, cold with its covering of dew and possessing a treacle-like sweetness.

The "top" fruits, apples, pears and plums require some sunlight on which to ripen their fruit and the new wood as it is formed.

APPLES. They should be grown as single cordons along a path or to hide a vegetable plot, or possibly to divide one part of the garden from another. Or they may be grown in horizontally trained form in tubs arranged around a courtyard. Owing to their susceptibility to red spider, apples should not be grown directly against a wall as for pears and plums. Not all varieties, however, prove suitable for restricted cultivation, some are of much too vigorous habit to keep in bounds and whilst certain varieties bear their fruit on short spurs, others form their fruit at the end of long shoots. These are the tip bearers, the most popular example being Worcester Pearmain which also makes a most vigorous tree and is therefore never successful when used in the artificial form. An exception to this is Lady Sudeley, which bears its handsome fruit on very short twigs and is of compact habit. It is never happier than in the restricted root run of a tub where it crops most heavily. As it is one of the earliest apples to mature it is much appreciated for tub culture. It also blooms later than most apples and so misses the frosts. Plant with it for pollination, Laxton's Superb or Sunset, both if possible, for they bloom together and will continue the supply of fruit until November. For Christmas dessert, plant either Claygate Pearmain or Adam's Pearmain. The first of these is self sterile and must have a pollinator, which may be one of those varieties mentioned. Its crisp, aromatic flavour is outstanding, equal to that of Cox's Orange Pippin which may also be grown in tubs with success. Of the hardy and free-cropping Adam's Pearmain, Lindley said that, "it possesses the best flavour of all apples". Where Cox's Orange proves difficult, the new Acme should be grown. It is the first dessert apple to crop on its own roots and will even set a heavy crop in its second year. It matures its deliciously flavoured fruit very late and if properly harvested will keep throughout winter. Where a cooking apple is required, the hardy Edward VII should be planted. The fruit, which is also pleasant eaten as dessert, will store until Lady Sudeley is ready the following August. Besides Worcester Pearmain, St. Cecilia, St. Edmund's Russet and Gladstone are tip bearers and are not suitable for growing in the artificial form, but almost all other apples with the exception of the most vigorous growers may be planted and it is chiefly the cookers which have a too vigorous habit, to which may be included Blenheim Orange and Belle de Boskoop. It is advisable, however, where training maiden trees, which is the most inexpensive method of planting apple trees, to obtain those which have been grown on a dwarfing rootstock. Either Malling IX or the new Malling-Merton (MM) 104 should be used for cordon or tub culture, for on these stocks, the trees will remain dwarf with the minimum of pruning and will come quickly into heavy bearing.

The single stem cordon should be planted 2 ft. apart where space is strictly limited and at an angle of 45° to restrict the vigour of the plant. Any time during the period November until March is the time to plant and where growing cordons in the open ground it will be advisable to fasten them to stout galvanized wires. These should be placed at intervals 6 in. apart, to a height of 5 ft. at which height the trees may ultimately be stopped.

The main stem is never pruned until it has reached the required height, but all lateral shoots must be regularly cut back to within 4–5 in. of the main stem to assist the formation of fruiting spurs. The time to do this is towards the end of August. Control of the spurs as they form will ensure successful crops and with established trees, wood formed from the spur during summer should be cut back to four buds during winter, lateral growth already having been stopped. From the point where the cut has been made laterals will form the second season, which in turn should be pinched back to two buds to enable the tree to concentrate its energies on the fruiting buds, whilst at the same time the balance between fruit and growth is maintained.

To train in the horizontal or espalier form, wires should also be used as previously suggested where growing from a maiden, though most gardeners will prefer to obtain their trees already trained. But to grow a tree in the horizontal form is in no way difficult and after planting, the main stem should be shortened to within 18 in. of soil level to a point where there are two buds close together on either side of the stem. The laterals to be formed by these buds should be tied to the wires on either side of the stem, first at an angle of 45°, then gradually brought to a horizontal position. The extension shoot of the main stem is allowed to grow away until two more buds appear 12–15 in. above the first pair when the leader is again cut back. The procedure continues until the wall is covered (as for pears) or where growing apples in tubs or in the open, until four or five horizontal arms have been formed, a new tier being formed each year. To encourage the tier branches to form fruiting spurs, all shoots must be pruned back in August to 4 in. of the main stem. Fruiting spurs are formed and maintained in the manner described for cordons. This pruning will occupy only a few minutes during summer and winter but must be carried out if heavy crops are to be enjoyed and the health of the tree maintained.

Whilst apples and pears enjoy soil conditions which are not in any way acid, an excess of lime is not required; indeed, heavy applications will be detrimental. Where planting in a town garden, give the ground a light dressing and incorporate some humus. As the apple requires magnesium in limited quantities, lime is best given as magnesium limestone or magnesium carbonate. Supplies of nitrogen and potash are also necessary for healthy growth, whilst if phosphorus is lacking, the fruit will be small. This may be given in the form of bone meal or steamed bone flour, 1 oz. being worked into the soil for the planting of each tree. Farmyard manure will provide both potash and nitrogen, but where this is not readily obtainable, potash may be given in the form of wood ash and nitrogen as shoddy or hop manure which should be worked deeply into the soil.

Planting should only be done when the soil is friable. If heavy, following rain or snow, or if containing frost, do not plant and remember that the younger the tree, the more readily will it transplant and become established. It is important to make the hole sufficiently large to take the roots without their being in any way bunched together and this is best ensured by making a small mound at the bottom of the hole round which the roots are spread. Soil, to which the manures have been mixed should be spread over the roots, treading it well down. Firm planting is most essential, the compost being trodden well down until the hole is filled in, taking care not to damage the stem of the tree with the boot or spade. The scion should be just above soil level after planting. Where planting against a wall as for pears and plums, additional humus should be given. This may be in the form of peat, lawn mowings or used hops which will also be valuable for using as a yearly mulch for all fruit trees. This additional humus will also be necessary where planting in tubs where the soil will tend to dry out more quickly. It is also important to provide ample drainage by way of crocks, over which should be placed a layer of turf turned upside down. When adding the soil and manures and it is not possible to tread, this should be rammed well down as the tub is filled to within 2 in. of the top. The space at the top is used for top dressing with strawy manure in early summer and to help the tubs to retain soil moisture, long straw or sacking which is kept moist, should be placed around the tubs during warm periods of mid-summer when the tubs should be watered as often as necessary.

Fertilization will be improved by artificially pollinating the flowers with a camel hair brush, for a town garden may be visited by few insects and bees. This should be done when the blooms are newly opening and when quite dry.

GOOSEBERRIES. The gooseberry crops heavily in the cordon or double cordon form and in this way may be grown in the most confined space, against a low wall, along a path or to divide one part of the garden from another. Cordon gooseberries are best planted in the open against wires, which should be fastened to stakes at 8-in. intervals, the stems being stopped when about 2 ft. 6 in. in height. Gooseberries are ideal plants for a walled garden situated in the north for the plants are always happiest in a cold, shaded position and will thrive under town conditions. All they ask for is a soil retaining moisture and some potash, which should be raked around the plants in spring each year at the rate of 2 oz. per square yard. An excess of nitrogen is not required, only sufficient to enable the plant to make new growth, for the gooseberry bears its fruit on both the old and the new wood and as a result crops most heavily. The gooseberry must have some humus in the soil to enable moisture to be retained during the often dry period of May and June so that the fruit will swell to a large size and be rich and juicy.

The single cordon is formed by growing on a rooted cutting to a single stem and pinching back all side shoots as they form. This is done in March, pinching back to 3 in. of their base. The double cordon is formed by cutting back the main stem to two buds 8–9 in. above the base of the stem. The shoots formed by the buds on either side the stem are trained to the wires, first at an angle of 45° then horizontally. This will be best done by tying the shoots to a short cane which may be gradually reduced to the horizontal position. When the shoots have 6–7 in. of wood on either side the stem, they should be stopped at a bud pointing in an upwards direction, all other buds being rubbed out. From here the upright cordons are formed and are treated in the same way as for single cordons. By the elimination of excessive wood, particularly old wood, and the restriction of the new shoots, the plant is able to concentrate its energies into the formation of large berries of exhibition quality. Single cordons should be planted 15 in. apart, double cordons being planted with their "leg" 18–20 in. apart.

Amongst the finest dessert varieties are Whitesmith and White Lion in the white section; with Broom Girl and High Sheriff outstanding yellows. Of green gooseberries, the olive-green Gunner and the huge oblong-shaped Thatcher are outstanding. For a late berry, the crimson-red Echo should be grown. Each of these varieties grow to a very large size and when mature will possess a flavour difficult to equal in any other fruit.

HYBRID BERRIES. To train up a wall, possibly the sunless wall of a town yard, a number of the not too vigorous hybrid berries may be expected to produce a heavy crop of fruit in autumn, in addition to proving attractive with their richly-coloured canes in winter and their orange and yellow leaves in autumn. They should be planted 6 ft. apart and require a soil well enriched with humus. They also require nitrogen to make plenty of new cane growth to displace the older wood as it forms, much of which should be cut out each winter.

Excellent for covering a wall is the Japanese Wineberry, its bright amber coloured fruit being borne on both the old and new wood, whilst its crimson canes, attractively covered with hairs remain colourful through winter. A delicious fruit is the Lowberry, the result of a cross between the blackberry and loganberry, its shining black fruit being nearly 2 in. in length and extremely sweet. The Thornless Loganberry is also excellent for a wall. It bears its mulberry coloured berries during July and August which, with its thornless canes presents no difficulty in its picking.

PEARS. Where the garden receives its fair share of sunshine and especially where they can be given the warmth of a sunny wall, pear trees should be planted, leaving the less favourable parts of the garden for apples and gooseberries. Pears are almost always grown in the horizontal form and planted against a wall they occupy little space. They should be planted on Quince "C" stock which comes quickly into bearing. The trees should always be planted with the scion or graft at least 3 in. above soil level, so that scion rooting cannot occur and with it the reduction in cropping.

The secret of growing good pears is to provide the trees with plenty of humus for they must have an abundance of moisture. Not only at planting time but each autumn afterwards. A liberal dressing of strawy manure or peat, augmented with fish manure or bone meal at the rate of 2 oz. per tree, should be lightly forked into the soil around the tree. A humus mulch should also be given in early summer. This should be spread around the tree and forked into the soil in autumn.

Careful choice should be made of varieties, for pears are more difficult than apples with their pollination. Conference will not pollinate Beurré d'Amanlis, nor will Seckle pollinate Louise Bonne. For early fruiting, Laxton's Superb is possibly the best pear ever introduced. It should be gathered towards the end of August and kept in a warm room for forty-eight hours before eating. It also blooms late and is valuable in frost troubled gardens. Plant with it Dr. Jules Guyot, another excellent all-round pear which blooms at the same time as Laxton's Superb and matures towards the end of September. For October, Laxton's Foremost, which crops well on a west wall, whilst for Christmas eating, Packham's Triumph, a new variety from New Zealand is proving quite outstanding. For late fruit, the old and hardy, Josephine Malines is still unbeatable.

PEACHES. The Peach requires protection from frost when in bloom, and needs plenty of sunshine to ripen its wood. In the British Isles it should be grown outdoors south of the Thames or in sheltered gardens of the west. Under glass it is grown against the high wall of a lean-to greenhouse and in a position of full sunlight. Fan-shaped trees should be planted in autumn, 18 ft. apart and in a soil containing lime (in the form of mortar) and enriched with slow-acting nitrogenous manures such as bone meal, given at a rate of 2 oz. per tree. This is incorporated into the soil at planting time. As with all grafted trees, make sure that the union is above soil level. Plant firmly and water well. During summer, keep the soil thoroughly moist and mulch with decaying manure or compost, for it is essential that the trees should not lack moisture whilst the fruit is swelling.

Peaches are propagated by budding on to plum stocks, the Common Mussel rootstock or Pershore stock making for vigorous medium-sized trees. The peach bears its fruit on shoots of the previous season's wood. During May, new growth formed by the leaders should be cut back by about one-third, whilst the tips of the side growths should be pinched out during midsummer, pinching them back when they are about 2 in. long. A single wood bud will be retained at the base of these shoots, to grow on as a replacement for next season's fruit, the shoot which has fruited being removed at the end of the season.

In the early years of the tree, pruning should take the same lines as for the renewal system for apples; that is, whilst the tree is being built up, the shoot which will have borne fruit is allowed to grow on until it has reached about 18 in. This is then fastened to the wall and the tip pinched back to a wood bud. It is the shoot formed from this bud that will bear the next season's crop.

It frequently happens that when building up a fan-shaped peach, that the branches or arms on one side are more vigorous than those of the other side. This should not be allowed to go unchecked, otherwise the balance of the tree will be completely spoilt. As it is known that the branches of the more horizontal shoots are less vigorous than those of a more vertical position, the shoots of the weaker side should be moved to a more vertical position whilst those on the more vigorous side should be fastened back more horizontally. In this position they should remain until growth has become more even.

It is not a difficult matter to distinguish between blossom and wood buds, the latter are small and pointed, whilst blossom buds are round and fat. Where possible select a wood bud facing the wall for an extension shoot for this will ensure a straighter shoot.

Peaches and nectarines will require more space in which to bear new wood than with either plums or sweet cherries.

Peaches grown as bush trees should be drastically pruned back in early May each year to encourage a continuous supply of new growth. This will stimulate growth which is excessive and should be retarded by ringing round the roots and cutting back in alternate years after the establishment of the trees.

The chief source of worry is the tendency of the plant to 'bleed' or 'gum', but this will not prove troublesome if not too much old wood is allowed to form. This, when pruned is most likely to 'gum', so it is advisable to encourage as much new wood as possible.

All shoots appearing next to a fruit should be pinched out above the second leaf. This removal of all unwanted shoots should be spread out over a period of three to four weeks early in summer.

Root pruning will also help to restrict excessive growth and encourage fruiting. About five years after planting, remove soil to a depth of 15 in. about 3–4 ft. from the main stem and, using a sharp knife, cut away all vigorous long roots before replacing the soil and treading firmly. Netting suspended from the wall hung over the trees when in bloom will give protection from frost.

Thinning should not be done until after 'stoning'. This is a natural falling off of fruits when about the size of a walnut. Those remaining should be 6 in. apart.

Alexander is one of the earliest varieties to ripen, it is a heavy cropper, bearing early in August medium-sized fruit of golden-yellow flushed with red; Barrington, one of the best for growing under glass in the British Isles, ripens towards the end of September, the large yellowish-green fruit being marked with crimson; Peregrine bears a large crimson fruit which ripens in August, and is a heavy and reliable cropper; Sea Eagle is the latest to ripen, being ready in October and it is one of the largest of all peaches, of pale yellow flushed with red.

PLUMS. With their vigorous habit, plums and gages are not in any way suitable for a small garden unless grown against a wall in the fan-shaped form. Owing to their bleeding when cut and the susceptibility of the trees to Silver Leaf disease, any pruning with plums should be done in early spring, when the wounds will then heal much more quickly than during winter and there will be less chance of the disease entering through the wound. Again, the tree will not lose vitality as it will where there is prolonged bleeding.

The fan-shaped tree is formed by cutting back the maiden to an upward bud, leaving below two buds which will form the first arms. After a season's growth, these in turn are pruned to within 15 in. of the main stem and it is from this point that the shoots are formed which are trained in the fan shape. The tree is built up as described for espalier apples and pears, the leader shoot being grown on each year when it is cut back to two more buds in March and so on, until the wall is covered with healthy growth. Cultural treatment will henceforth consist of cutting back the new wood to two-thirds of that formed. This should be done in May and to encourage fruiting, side growths should also be cut back to within 3 in. of the base.

For those walls which may be clothed only in ugly ivy which may be damaging to the structure of the property, plums and pears should be grown as an alternative, utilizing the southerly wall for pears and those facing east or west for plums. To be successful grown against a wall, a plum tree must receive an abundance of moisture about the roots and the plum must be given almost as liberal a quantity of nitrogen as the black currant. This is best given in the form of long strawy manure which will also provide the moisture-holding humus. Owing to their high moisture requirements, plums generally crop best in a heavy soil, provided it is well drained. Where of a light, sandy nature, liberal quantities of humus should be given each year as a mulch after fruiting. Where farmyard manure cannot be obtained, incorporate wool shoddy, or peat augmented by 1 oz. of sulphate of ammonia to each tree. This should be given during spring, when any pruning is done.

INDEX